Simplify Your Life

ALSO BY ELAINE ST. JAMES

Inner Simplicity

Living the Simple Life

Simplify Your Life with Kids

Simplify
Your Life

100 Ways to Slow Down and
Enjoy the Things That Really Matter

Elaine St. James

HYPERION
New York

Book design by Richard Oriolo

Library of Congress Cataloging-in-Publication Data
St. James, Elaine.
Simplify your life : 100 ways to slow down and enjoy the things
that really matter / Elaine St. James.
p.   cm.
ISBN 0-7868-8000-7
1. Simplicity. I. Title.
BJ1496.S7 1994
646.7—dc20   93-27749
                                        CIP
                                        Rev

Gift Edition
ISBN: 0-7868-6345-5

1 3 5 7 9 10 8 6 4 2

To Wolcott Gibbs, Jr.

And to Michelle and Bill, Jessie and Megan,
and Lisa and Eric

∽

To Sarah
Something to Read then Something to Do
To A Great Friend

Love Trudy

1999

Acknowledgments

I'd like to thank Marcia Burtt, Dave Sowle, Marisa Kennedy Miller, Jackie Powers, Judy Babcock, Phil Babcock, Jim Cummings, Meg Torbert, Linda Miller, Albert Chiang, and Ira Weinstein for their support and encouragement in the writing of this book. I'd like to thank Felix Fusco, Sue Pettengill, Cyndy Van der Poel, Hope Kores, Kathy McDonough, Beverly Brennan, my mother, Dorothy Kennedy, and my favorite aunt, Kathleen Schiffler, for always being there. I'd like to thank Sam Vaughan for his advice and inspiration, and for connecting me with my wonderful agent, Jane Dystel. And most of all, I'd like to thank my husband, Wolcott Gibbs, Jr., for everything.

Contents

∽

Two: Your Life-Style

Three: Your Finances

Four: Your Job

Five: Your Health

Six: Your Personal Life

Seven: Special Issues for Women

Eight: Hard-Core Simplicity

Simplify Your Life

Introduction

∽

Let your boat of life be light, packed with only what you need—a homely home and simple pleasures, one or two friends worth the name, someone to love and someone to love you, a cat, a dog, and a pipe or two, enough to eat and enough to wear, and a little more than enough to drink, for thirst is a dangerous thing.

—Jerome Klapka Jerome

Several years ago I was sitting at my desk, idly glancing at my daily schedule, which was laid out in a time-management system roughly the size of Nebraska. This binder was bursting with "to-do" lists, phone logs, time-organizers, meeting-maximizers, goal-stabilizers, high-tech efficiency charts, and five- and ten-year life planners. Suddenly, I realized I no longer wanted my life to be that complicated.

I immediately picked up the phone and scheduled a long

weekend retreat. I left my time-management system at home, but I took a notebook. I had a lot of thinking to do.

Like many others of our generation, my husband, Gibbs, and I had bought into the Bigger is Better and the More is Better Yet philosophies of the 1980s. We had the big house, the big car, most of the conveniences, and many of the toys of the typical yuppie life-style. Then we gradually began to realize that, rather than contributing to our lives, many of these things complicated them far more than we had been willing to admit. We had always known the Joneses weren't worth keeping up with, but we finally had to face the fact that the only thing we'd ever gotten from a power lunch was indigestion. The time had come for us to get off the fast track.

Over the next few days I sat alone in the peaceful silence of that retreat house, and came up with a list of things we could do to improve the quality of our lives while decreasing the complexity. When I got home, I sat down with Gibbs and went over the list. Fortunately, he agreed with all of the major and most of the minor changes I proposed.

The first thing we did was get rid of all the stuff we didn't use anymore (#1). We took a giant step and moved across country, so we could work where we wanted to live (#51), and do what we really wanted to do (#52). In the process we moved to a smaller house (#19). Over the next few years we

simplified our eating habits (#57), consolidated our investments (#46), sold the damn boat (#21), rethought our
buying habits (#40), and drastically reduced our needs for
goods and services (#42). Step by step, we gradually imple-
mented most of the ideas outlined in this book.

When we launched our simplicity program, we had three
specific goals in mind. First, we wanted the things in our
lives—our home, our cars, our clothes, our diets, our finances—to be small enough and few enough and simple
enough that we could easily take care of them *ourselves*.

Second, we wanted to free ourselves from the commitments, the people, and the obligations that kept us from
having time to do the things we really want to do. We made
the decision early on to stop doing the things that we'd always
done because we felt we *should* do them. Not only has this
increased the time we have for ourselves, but it has greatly
reduced the stress that comes from doing things we don't
want to do.

Third, we wanted our lives to be consistent with our desire
to live in harmony with the environment.

For us, simplifying was not the "going back to the land"
movement of the 1960s—though we did want to include
more nature in our lives, and we have. Nor was it about living
cheaply, though close to half of the suggestions in this book

will reduce your expenditures. For us, living simply meant reducing the scale, maintaining the comfort, eliminating the complexity, and minimizing the time demands of life as we had known it in the 1980s.

When we first started to simplify, I longed for guidance from others who had been there before us. I combed libraries and bookstores in search of help. While a fair amount has been written about the *philosophy* of the simple life, I was unable to find anything of a *practical* nature that outlined specific things we could do to simplify. So we plodded along on our own.

Each time we completed a major step in our simplification process, we discovered some other minor things we could do to simplify, and we added them to our list. I decided that if the two of us—for the most part rational and reasonable people—had gotten so caught up in the frenetically paced lifestyle and rampant consumerism of the eighties, there must be other reasonable people out there who had done the same thing, and who were now looking for practical things they could do to simplify their lives. And so I decided to write this book, which is a compilation of those steps we've taken to simplify, and the things we've learned from other like-minded people along the way.

It's possible your life is complicated enough—as ours was—to warrant implementing many or all of these suggestions. Or, it might be that taking just one or two of these steps—like cleaning up your relationships (#72), or changing your expectations (#88)—will provide the level of simplicity you need to more fully enjoy the other areas of your life. Whatever the case, keep in mind that one person's simplicity is another's complexity. Bowing out of the holidays (#33) was tremendously liberating for us, but it might complicate your life beyond words. You get to decide.

Wise men and women in every major culture throughout history have found that the secret to happiness is not in getting more but in wanting less. The nineties appear to be presenting one of those golden moments of change, the opportunity to freely give up the things that don't make us happy and to incorporate the lessons of the eighties into a simple but elegant life-style for the nineties—and into the next century. So, to paraphrase Henry David Thoreau, take advantage of the movement of the times and simplify, simplify. And enjoy.

One

Your Household

1. Reduce the Clutter in Your Life

∽

A giant step on the road to simplicity is to eliminate the odds and ends that clutter up your home, your car, your office, and your life. If you're moving to a smaller home (#19), paring down will no doubt be a necessity. As you start your program to reduce the clutter, the guideline is easy: *If you haven't used it in a year or more, get rid of it.*

Getting rid of it can mean any number of things: give it to a friend, give it to Goodwill, take it to a consignment shop, sell it at a garage sale, or put it in the Dumpster.

Start with your clothes closets and branch out from there. Clean out every closet, every drawer, every shelf, in every room of your house, including the kitchen. Do you really need a full-sized Cuisinart *and* a mini-Cuisinart *and* a handheld chopper *and* a·mixer? (See #35 for some ideas on how to get rid of these things.) Don't forget the front hall closet, the linen closet, tool chests, and the medicine cabinets. (See #66; it will save you a lot of time trying to decide what to keep.) Remember the laundry room, the garage, the attic, the basement, your office, your car, and any storage space you may be renting or borrowing.

When Gibbs and I started to simplify, we went through this exercise and were amazed at the amount of "stuff" we had accumulated that we simply didn't use anymore. Getting rid of it all was a tremendously liberating experience.

Soon after that, we came to the realization that we really had far more living space than we actually needed or even wanted, so we moved from our house to a small condominium. In the process of moving, we went through a second uncluttering exercise, and managed to free ourselves from another load of things we would no longer have room for.

We've found, as we've refined our simplification program over the past couple of years, that we're getting better and better at letting go of the things we know we'll never use again. You may not be ready to get rid of everything in your closets on the first uncluttering round or two, but I promise that once you begin to experience the exhilaration and the sense of freedom such an exercise generates, uncluttering will become easier and easier.

You can complete the initial stage of an unclutter program in a couple of Saturday afternoons. Be sure to have your children go through this exercise with you. It's a great way for them to learn at an early age how to keep their lives uncluttered. Just schedule the time and get started.

Remember, the idea is not to deny yourself the things you want, but to free yourself from the things you don't want.

2. Use Dave's Uncluttering System

~

Our friend Dave swears by this method for getting rid of things he no longer needs, but can't bear to throw out: Put them in a box with a label indicating a date two or three years from now—but don't list the contents on the label. Store the box in the attic or the basement, or wherever is convenient. Once a year, examine the labels. When you come across a box whose date has passed, throw it out without opening it. Since you don't know what's inside, you'll never miss it.

Of course, it's much easier to keep your life free of clutter if you make it a habit not to hoard in the first place. You can stop things from accumulating by getting in the habit of throwing them out now, rather than later. Every time you start to store something in the back of your closet or in a dark attic, ask yourself, "Do I *really* want to save this, or will it end up adding to the clutter?" Then discipline yourself to throw it out now.

3. Use "Speed Cleaning" to Clean Your House

✧

If you've reduced your needs for goods and services (#42), you may already have let the cleaning lady go. But, whether you clean your house yourself or hire someone to do it for you, you should read *Speed Cleaning,* by Jeff Campbell and the Clean Team (available from Dell Publishing). You can read it in less than thirty minutes and it will cut your housecleaning time and expense by more than half.

I consider myself fairly efficient, but I'd never even thought of some of the simple time-saving techniques described in this book. For example, easy-to-follow, step-by-step diagrams show you exactly how to set up the cleaning process for your home, room by room, so you can move from top to bottom and from left to right, all the way around a room and the entire house *without backtracking.* This tip alone will reduce your cleaning time drastically.

It's actually possible for one person using the Speed Cleaning system to thoroughly clean a 1,200-square-foot house in little more than an hour. Once you have set up your home for speed cleaning, you don't *have* to do the cleaning every week:

these methods are so thorough that cleaning every other week or even once a month—depending on your circumstances—will suffice.

The book shows you how to save time, energy, water, cleaning supplies, and, best of all, your Saturdays. It discusses environmentally safe products and the latest tools and cleaning techniques. It even shows you how to get the best from your cleaning service.

It might seem that letting the cleaning lady go would complicate rather than simplify your life, and, if you've got a five-bedroom house, it probably would. But if you're moving toward a human-scale, low-maintenance life-style, you can easily take care of the routine cleaning without outside help, especially if you include all the family members in the process. Teaching your children efficient cleaning and household maintenance techniques will not only make your life easier, but will give them skills for keeping their own lives simple.

4. Cut Your Grocery Shopping Time in Half

✑

Most people I know find themselves running to the super-market at least two or three times a week, and many shop more often than that.

One extreme case is a friend of mine who shops for food every day of the week. She is a married career woman with no children who spends close to a thousand dollars a month on food for herself and her husband. Though she claims to detest shopping, she has never got herself organized enough to plan ahead for meals and for grocery buying. (Her excuse is that she wants to be sure her produce is fresh every day. As I see it, that's what refrigerators are for.) Consequently, she spends far more time, money, and energy on shopping than neces-sary, and she ends up throwing out an unbelievable amount of food because she buys on impulse things she doesn't really want or need.

When we started our simplification program, one of the first things I looked at was how I could simplify our grocery shopping chore, since dawdling in a food store is one of my least favorite ways to spend time. I made it a goal to cut by at least half the two or three hours I spent shopping each week.

So I sat down at the computer and typed up a list of all the food items I might possibly buy. Then I arranged them in the order they appear in the aisles of my favorite grocery store. I ran off a couple dozen copies of the list, which I keep in one of the kitchen cabinets so a fresh one is there when I need it. It can easily be updated as our eating patterns change.

Now, before I go shopping, I sit down at the kitchen table and draw up a quick meal plan for the week. Then I go through my computer list and check off the items I'll need. Since I'm right there in the kitchen, I can quickly see what we're out of, and note those items on the list.

The entire process, from making the list to doing the shopping to putting the groceries away, takes a little less than an hour, and I almost never have to run back to the store during the week for items I've forgotten. Of course, we've also simplified our eating habits (#57), but, just by keeping a list, we've substantially cut our monthly food expenditure, and created more free time for ourselves.

Another advantage of using a computerized list is that if you're the primary shopper and have to be away on shopping day, it's very easy for your mate or one of your kids to check off the list and take care of the shopping in your absence.

5. Buy in Bulk

Another way to simplify your grocery shopping is to buy in bulk. For years I resisted this idea. We never seemed to have the storage space, and I just never took the time to sit down and figure out what we could buy in large quantities. Then, when we started making our own oat bran muffins (#61), we went through so much oat bran it became much easier to buy it in bulk.

When I saw what buying oat bran this way saved in time and energy and packaging—not to mention money—I began to think about other things I could buy in quantity. I was surprised at how extensive the list was. Now, I have a separate list for our bulk purchases: paper towels, Kleenex, detergents, cleansers, pet foods, toothpaste, shampoos, shaving creams, rice, grains, legumes, nuts, and baking supplies.

Once or twice a year I make a trip to our local wholesale house to stock up on these items. Since we've eliminated so much of the clutter in our closets and cabinets (#1), we have plenty of room to keep these supplies on hand, and we never run out of things we need.

When buying in bulk keep in mind that not *everything* offered at a wholesale market is necessarily less expensive, so you should have a good idea of regular prices on the items you wish to purchase. Otherwise, you could end up paying too much. While cost savings is only one of the advantages of buying in bulk, why pay more than you have to? Secondly, you'll find it much easier to shop for bulk items with a detailed list; otherwise there's an overwhelming temptation to buy things you don't really need but that you can't pass up because the price is so good.

In addition to the time and money we've saved, one of the most rewarding benefits of buying in bulk is the reduction in packaging materials to be recycled. In fact, many wholesale houses, especially cooperatives, encourage customers to bring their own shopping bags and containers, which reduces packaging materials even more.

6. Plant a Garden

≈

We have friends who have simplified their grocery shopping by planting a garden. Their entire yearly crop is raised
in planters on their front deck. They have fresh tomatoes,
peppers, green beans, artichokes, cucumbers, and several
types of squash, as well as an extensive herb garden. They've
set up a drip irrigation system on an automatic timer. They
never have to till the soil; when a crop is finished, they pull
out the old plant, add some fresh mulch, and put in a new
one. The planters are on wheels so they can be rotated easily
to get the maximum sun through the season. They seldom
have to spray for bugs, but when they do they use an organic
mixture of one part detergent to ten parts water.

They're professionals who both work long hours. They
decided some years ago they'd rather spend time on their
deck tending their plants than running to the market every
time they need a tomato. They get a tremendous amount of
satisfaction from being the source of much of the produce that
goes on their table, not the least of which comes from the fact
that it is organically grown. What little work they do to tend

this simple garden gives them a lot of enjoyment, and they love the feeling of being in touch with nature. Also, they've made a point of involving their teenage son in their gardening routine. Not only has he been a big help to them, but he has developed an appreciation for plants and nature he might not otherwise have had. And they've come to treasure the opportunity to work together as a family at an activity they all enjoy.

If you have the space for a deck or patio garden, planting one might not only simplify your grocery shopping, but add a great deal of satisfaction to your life as well.

7. Run All Your Errands in One Place

‿

I used to spend an inordinate amount of time doing my routine errands. Each week, without giving it a second thought, I drove all over town to my favorite little shops, which I patronized more out of habit than convenience. I would drive seven miles to one side of town for groceries, five miles back into town to the bank, two blocks away to the post office, another six miles to the opposite side of town for the dry cleaners, and then to a shopping center several miles beyond that, where I took care of almost everything else: video rental, hardware store, bookstore, and pet supplies. And, of course, don't forget another short drive to stop at the fish market, the bakery, and the flower stall.

Now, fortunately, we live within one block of a shopping area where we can take care of everything in one stop, and also have the vet and the pet groomer, a photo lab, a pharmacy, and even a half dozen good restaurants we can walk to. It has cut at least an hour and a half off the time it takes to do our weekly errands.

If you don't live in close proximity to a shopping center

where you can take care of all your weekly shopping needs, find the one closest to you and drive there, even if it's halfway across town, for the simplicity of one-stop shopping.

The automobile, like the washer and dryer (#8), is another convenience we tend to misuse. Because it's so easy to hop in and drive away, we don't think about all the extra time we spend doing things we wouldn't do, and maybe don't really *need* to do, if we didn't have the car that makes it so "easy."

8. Cut Your Laundering Chore in Half

∽

In his excellent book *Timelock,* Ralph Keyes points out that there are many supposedly time-saving devices that, because of the way we use them, don't save us as much time as we think they do. The automatic washer and dryer are perfect examples.

Studies have been conducted over the past fifty years comparing the time our grandmothers and mothers spent on certain chores with the time we spend on them today. It's interesting to see that even though our washers and dryers greatly reduce the amount of time it takes to clean and dry a load of clothes, we're spending just as much time on the clothes washing chore as our grandmothers did, and in some cases more. Why? Because we're doing more loads.

In the old days, for example, Grandpa would put on a clean shirt on Monday and, after wearing it carefully through the end of the week, it would go into the clothes hamper for Grandma to take care of on wash day. Now we think nothing of wearing two or three shirts a day, one for exercise, one for work, one for casual wear, and throwing them into the laundry basket the minute we take them off.

The same is true of towels and linens. Today, without batting an eye, we use a towel or maybe two or three per person per day. After all, it's so easy: just run another load through the machine, right?

It's one thing if you have household help to do the laundry, though there is still the water, the detergent, the gas, the electricity, and the expense to think about, not to mention having to supervise the help; but it's another matter entirely if you're the one doing the laundry, and you're spending far more time each week in the laundry room than you want or need to.

If that's the case, sit down and rethink your use of clothes and other launderable items. An easily attainable goal would be to cut back your laundry to the equivalent of one load per person per week. After you've done that for a while, it'll be easy to cut back again, to one load every two weeks, especially once you've simplified your wardrobe (#22), and have mostly dark colors that don't need to be laundered so often! Wear your clothes to the max and teach your kids to do the same. Assign one towel and one washcloth per person per week.

And who says we have to change the sheets *every* week? Our mothers did because it was the accepted way then. But, with so many mothers working outside the home, in addition to also working in the home, things are different now. I'm here to tell you it's possible to go for two weeks (or more) without changing the sheets on your bed and live to tell about it. Just don't tell my mother.

9.   Stop Buying Clothes That Need to Be Dry-Cleaned

Obviously, there are a number of occupations with dress codes requiring clothes that must be regularly dry-cleaned. If you're an investment banker, you have to have your three-piece suits, which don't respond well to being run through the washer and dryer. Fortunately, most of us in the 1990s no longer need to be slaves to the Dress for Success code that ruled the 1980s. From now on, at least until the Revolution, the code should be Dress for Comfort and Convenience, which means, for the most part, wash-and-wear cottons and natural fabrics.

I have a friend who argues that taking a load of clothes to the cleaners is much simpler than having to run a comparable amount of clothes through the laundry, and for some that may be true. It comes down to a life-style choice, and how simple you want your life to be. For years we made weekly trips to the dry cleaners to pick up the shirts and to drop off the week's cleaning, and never gave it a second thought. Now that we've simplified our wardrobe, it's much easier to avoid the dry cleaners. I love being able to run a load of clothes through the washer/dryer, hang them up, and know they're ready to wear. And we take some satisfaction in knowing that we've reduced, even if only by a small fraction, the use of environmentally harmful dry-cleaning solvents.

10. Leave Your Shoes at the Front Door

⌒

Get in the habit of removing your shoes before you enter your house. This simple practice has some incredible benefits. By reducing the amount of outdoors that is brought indoors, you reduce the amount of dust and other unwelcome particles on the carpet and the floors. Your house will be visibly cleaner: dirt stains on the carpets and rugs are kept to a minimum, carpets are much easier to keep clean, and the overall dust quotient throughout the house is greatly reduced.

But perhaps the greatest benefit for the simplicity-oriented is that taking off your street shoes at the front door helps to create the sense of your home as a sanctuary. It's almost magical: when you leave your shoes at the door, you start to feel you can leave your troubles there, too.

A variation on this idea comes from an acquaintance who owns a computer software firm. Because of the importance of creating a dust-free environment in his workplace, he started many years ago requiring his employees to leave their shoes outside. He even went so far as to buy each employee shoes or slippers to be worn indoors and maintains a shoe budget for his staff. His employees and visitors are trained from day one to check their shoes at the door.

Hint: Build or create (or, as a last resort, purchase) a small box or rack where you can leave your shoes when you come into your home. Keep a supply of socks or your slippers there if you're the type who has to have something on your feet. Also, keep some extra socks or a supply of airline slipper-socks for guests, and encourage them to leave their shoes at the door, too.

11.   Go for Patterned Carpets

ℴ

When I think back to the time I decided to have light taupe carpet installed in our newly remodeled home, I wonder why I didn't have my head examined. It was the mid-eighties, and the taupe and gray and off-white carpets were a fashionable rebellion against the dark brown and orange shags of the seventies, and possibly even the sculpted greens of the sixties.

Yes, the light, low plush carpets are fashionable and, if well maintained, look beautiful, but simple they ain't. They show every spot, every fleck of dirt, every cat hair, every crumb of toast, and every slosh of coffee that ever passed over their supposedly stain-resistant fibers.

When we moved from our house into the condo, I replaced the light carpet that was there with a multicolored flecked carpet that looks like sand. It was the best decorating decision I ever made. There are many such patterned carpets available today, and if you find yourself changing carpets, I strongly urge you to consider one. Or, consider a multicolored Persian or Oriental rug that will achieve the same results. It's not that they stay so much cleaner, it's simply that they don't *show* the spots, the specks, the drips, the dust, and the smudges as easily as the plain light-colored ones, or even the solid-colored dark ones, for that matter. If you want your carpets to look good without having to spend a lot of time on them, a speckled or patterned or multicolored carpet will hide a multitude of sins and will make your life a whole lot easier.

12. Use Food Trays

∽

When I went on my private retreat at the beginning of our simplification program, I spent a wonderfully quiet and refreshing weekend in a beautiful old stone house up in the hills. The house comfortably accommodates anywhere from eight to ten guests at a time and is usually booked months in advance. Guests can have their meals in the communal dining room, or can take meals to their rooms. Coffee, teas, fruit drinks, and all manner of non-dietetic, drippy, crumbly, gooey snacks are available all day long. Guests laden with these spillable foodstuffs make regular treks across carpeted hallways, up and down polished stone stairways, through rooms covered with gorgeous Persian and Oriental carpets, and over beautifully maintained hardwood floors. Yet the floors and carpets and rugs are spotless.

Why? There is only one rule in the house: Any food or drink leaving the kitchen has to be on a tray. When I think of all the time I used to spend blotting up spills from the light taupe carpet and brushing crumbs off the hardwood floors, I wonder why I never thought of this myself. We now have one rule in our house regarding food: Any food or drink leaving the kitchen has to be on a tray. It is such a simple, and elegant, solution.

13. Keep Your Plants
Outdoors

Have you ever lifted one of your houseplants to move it to a sunnier spot, and found a ten-inch-diameter water stain on your newly refinished hardwood floor?

Is your coffee table spotted with water marks that were made when you failed to notice the base of the planter holding your favorite orchid had overflowed?

Do you find yourself looking at the philodendron hanging over the kitchen sink and wondering when you'll ever have the time to take it down and dust the leaves?

Are you tired of brushing against the ficus next to the couch and dislodging another layer of dead leaves to litter the carpet?

How often do you come home to find your cat has thrown up on your sofa again because she's been eating the schefflera?

Interior decorators and serious plant lovers won't like this idea, but the rest of you know what I mean: houseplants are a pain in the neck. It's time we realized that the photographs in the home-and-garden magazines don't necessarily reflect reality. They make having indoor plants look so easy, when they're anything but. And I'm speaking from years of being a plant lover, surrounded by indoor plants that took up a lot of my time. It was the water ring on the cherrywood bookcase and the third infestation of aphids on my flowering hibiscus that made me think there might be a better way to get in touch with nature.

If you don't have a yard or a patio where you can enjoy natural greenery, consider a window box. If that's not possible, visit your local botanical garden or neighborhood park when you need a plant fix. At the very least, don't replace your Creeping Charlie next time it dies. You'll be amazed at how simple your life can become when you keep nature outdoors where God intended it to be.

14. Get Rid of Your Lawn

~

Unless you're one of those weekend wonders whose passion is huffing and puffing behind a push lawn mower, or worse yet, walking behind a noisy, smelly, environmentally damaging, pollutant-spewing power mower, why would you have grass in your yard? Neighborhood custom? Social expectations? Habit? Do you really *like* having a lawn? Is it worth having to keep it trimmed, clipped, mowed, fertilized, aerated, raked, and watered?

Even if you have someone else, such as a hired gardener, to take care of your lawn for you, you still have to expend the effort to get it done; at the very least you have to write the check for the work. Wouldn't it be simpler to get rid of your lawn altogether?

You could save a great deal of time, money, effort, energy, water, and other natural resources (gas or electricity for the mower), as well as unnatural resources (chemical fertilizers and weed killers), by replacing your lawn with ground cover.

Many beautiful, drought-tolerant, fast-growing, low-maintenance ground covers—pachysandra, dichondra, ivy, and numerous low-growing evergreens, for example—are available as effective lawn replacements. Check with your nurseryman for the one best suited to your locale.

Imagine never again having to concern yourself with a lawn. Just get rid of it.

15. At the Very Least, Simplify Your Lawn Maintenance

⁓

If you feel you absolutely have to have a lawn, consider making some changes in the way you keep it:

1. Make it smaller—just enough space for the kids to wrestle with the dog.

2. Most people overwater their lawns by up to 40 percent. Remember to water slowly and deeply. This is more effective than shorter, frequent sprinklings. The best time to water is early morning.

3. Mow it less frequently. Not only does this save time and energy, but most types of grass develop healthier roots when allowed to grow up to two or three inches high. The longer the grass, the more shade for the ground around each plant. This helps the soil retain the moisture longer, which in turn means less watering.

4. Don't rake the grass clippings. Leaving them on the lawn not only saves you time and energy, it helps to retain the moisture and creates a natural fertilizer for the grass. Also,

recycling the mowed grass into your own lawn reduces the amount of clippings that are added to your local landfill.

5. If you must use pesticides, use organic rather than chemical ones.

16. Pets Simplified

The second year into our simplicity program Gibbs brought home a little Shih Tzu puppy. Though we have two very low maintenance cats, neither of us had ever had a dog before. We didn't have a clue what we were in for.

One evening at the end of the first week, we sat and watched in amazement as Piper ran around chewing on everything in sight, messing up the carpet, terrorizing the cats, and generally creating havoc in our peaceful home. Gibbs looked at me and said, "Maybe we overdid the simplicity bit." Had our lives gotten so simple that we had to bring in this little ball of fur to stir things up?

Well, perhaps. But what it came down to is that we'd finally simplified our lives enough so we could enjoy the pleasures, and put up with the hassles, of owning a dog, something we'd never had time to do before.

Pets won't simplify your life, but there are things you can do to make pet ownership easier:

1. Unless you love pet grooming, stick with short-haired pets. Even with short-haired animals, take a few minutes each day to brush your cat or dog; this reduces the amount of hair that ends up in your carpet, or as fur balls on the hardwood floor.

2. If at all possible, keep your pets indoors. Obviously, this is easier with small dogs than with large ones. But indoor pets are much less likely to get into fights with other animals (requiring expensive and time-consuming trips to the vet), and the chance of them being hit by a car (which can be not only expensive but fatal), is greatly reduced. Also, indoor pets have fewer problems with fleas.

3. If your pets do have fleas, the best method for getting rid of them (both in the house and on your pets) is Flea Busters (1-800-767-FLEA). This is an environmentally safe, simple, nontoxic method guaranteed to rid your house and your pets of fleas for up to one year. Most pet stores offer a product similar to that used by Flea Busters that you can use yourself at considerable savings.

4. Take the time to train your dog. Whether you have a new puppy or an older dog, all dogs can be trained to obey basic commands such as COME, SIT, STAY, HEEL, QUIET, and STOP CHEWING ON THAT TABLE LEG! Contrary to what many veterinarians will tell you, puppies can start basic train-

ing at three months (and house training should start the minute you bring them home). Call your local Humane Society for information on training classes in your community.

A well-trained dog, while not simple, can be a true joy to have in your life. Because of Piper, we make absolutely certain that we take our brisk walk every day (#63). And, taking her out at first light in the morning and the last thing at night has brought us in closer touch with nature. We now regularly see many phases of the moon and stars that we hadn't seen before, and the quiet sights and sounds and smells of dawn and night are special gifts that we've come to enjoy every day of the year.

17. Moving Simplified

We've moved eight times in fifteen years. Here are some things we learned along the way:

1. Before you move, go through the uncluttering exercise outlined in #1.

2. Most people start packing long before they need to. As a result, the house looks like a disaster area for weeks before the actual move. The average household can be packed up in less than a week. If you hire movers to do the packing, it can usually be done in one day, but get an estimate from them as to how long they will take. Set aside one room in the house in which packed boxes can be kept out of the way while you are packing up.

3. When packing, start with treasures such as vases and art objects (of course, these are now going into the mathom box, #35); then do books, linens, clothes, and personal items. Pack the kitchen last, preferably on the morning of the move while the movers are loading everything else into the van.

4. Make sure the place you are moving to is cleaned and ready to live in.

5. Set up a system of colored labels for the movers to use. All boxes with red labels go to the kitchen, all boxes with blue labels go to the living room, etc.

6. If you're moving across town, move the kitchen things you'll need for your next couple of meals—dinner tonight and breakfast in the morning—the clothes you'll need, and an overnight kit, in your own car. These will be the things you'll unpack first.

7. Use the large wardrobe boxes for your clothes, and load them directly from the closet in the old place into the closets in the new place. If you've simplified your wardrobe (#22), you'll have little to pack.

8. When packing books, start with the top shelf of a bookcase, and move from left to right all the way down to the bottom shelf. Take a stack from the shelf and put them right into the box in the same order. Label the boxes by bookcase and by number. Don't worry about filling every square inch of space in the box. You may use a few more boxes this way, but it is so much simpler.

Instruct the movers to set up the bookcases in the new house, and to stack the book boxes next to them in numerical order. Start with box number one, and stack the books on the shelves exactly as you packed them, in the same order.

9. Whenever possible, use a mover who'll sell you boxes and then will take them back at half price. Many moving companies also sell used boxes at considerable savings.

10. Board pets and young children for the day. Older kids can help with the unpacking of their personal things.

11. Draw up a rough schematic showing the rooms in the new house and where you'd like the furniture to be placed. Run off enough copies so you can post one copy on the door of each room. This will save you from having to be on the spot each time the movers bring in a piece of furniture or a stack of boxes. That means you can be in the kitchen unpacking and organizing for dinner that evening, or at least for breakfast in the morning.

18. Recycling Simplified

One of the wonderful side benefits of simplifying your life is how easy the process of recycling becomes. By simplifying your eating habits (#57), you'll greatly reduce the packaging that automatically comes with processed foods. By making water your drink of choice (#60), you'll greatly reduce the number of cans, bottles, and plastic containers you have to dispose of. By eliminating the daily newspaper (#28), cutting back on your magazine subscriptions (#27), and stopping your junk mail (#26), you'll greatly reduce the amount of paper you have to recycle.

You'll also cut back on bottles and packaging by throwing out everything but the aspirin, and by reducing your use of prescription and over the counter remedies that don't work (#66). Rethinking your buying habits (#40) and your need for goods and services (#42), and bowing out of the holidays (#33) will reduce not only the packaging, but also the number of items that clutter up your life. And of course, uncluttering (#1), staying uncluttered (#89), and gift-giving simplified (#35) are automatic recycling processes in themselves.

Experts agree that for all its promises, recycling is only a part of the world's waste disposal problem. Reducing waste in the first place, which simplifying will do, will be a major part of the solution.

T w o

Your Life-Style

19. Move to a Smaller House

How has it happened that the size of the average American home has gone from the roughly 900-square-foot, two-bedroom, one-bath home of the 1950s to a roughly 2,000-square-foot home with three bedrooms, three and a half baths, an eat-in kitchen, a dining room, a library, an exercise room, a "great" room, a TV room, at least a two- but often a three-car garage, and an entry hall that rivals the size of the Sistine Chapel? It certainly did not happen because of the need to house larger families; the average family size has gone from 4 in the 1950s to 2.5 in the 1990s.

The monthly financial burden of maintaining these behemoths has more than doubled, and in many cases tripled, from the 1950s. Today, many homeowners are spending more than half their monthly income on housing. In order to have larger houses, we've had to move farther and farther away from our jobs and community services. This in turn means we have to spend more time commuting and more money on gas and cars.

Many people are beginning to realize that what they've had

to give up in terms of time, energy, and money to own a large house is just not worth it.

When Gibbs and I moved from the smog and the congestion and the four-hour commutes of the big city and suburbs to a more rural environment where we could live where we worked (#51), our first move was into a 3,000-square-foot house. We'd unwittingly bought into the eighties mentality that bigger is better. Besides, we needed that space to house all our stuff.

Once we had got rid of the stuff (#1), we realized we no longer needed all that space. When we moved to our small condominium, our goal was to scale down to easily manageable size in our accommodations, without loss of comfort or conveniences. It's been a tremendous emotional and psychological relief not to have to worry about that big house, the big yard, and the ever increasing complexities of owning an oversized home that no longer fits our life-style.

20. Drive a Simple Car

∽

When it comes to simplicity in the car department, Gibbs and I are partway there.

A few years back, in typically upwardly mobile fashion, I bought one of those high-powered foreign sedans. While it has for the most part been a reliable car and, for me, a real joy to drive, it would be a stretch to call it simple. It's a fair amount of trouble and expense to maintain, I have to be careful where I park it, and the gas consumption—26 miles to the gallon in town—is difficult to justify in this day of 50-mpg cars.

Gibbs, on the other hand, has a ten-year-old Plymouth. He grew up in New York City on subways and buses and never even owned a car until he moved to the suburbs. Then he bought an old station car that barely made it back and forth to the train. Unlike me, he has absolutely no ego tied up in the car he drives. For him, a car is a sometimes convenient means for getting from one place to another.

The insurance and taxes and registration fees on his car are half of what they are on mine. He can take his car anywhere and not have to worry about it being broken into or stolen. (As he is the first to admit, no one would want it.)

My car is in the shop nearly twice as often as his. Even the smallest part costs three times what it would for his car, and often takes twice as long to get.

Recently, after experimenting with our local bus service, Gibbs found it quite adequate for his needs, and, like our friends in San Francisco (#96), he is seriously considering getting rid of his car altogether. In addition to reducing his transportation expenses by two-thirds, it would relieve him of the task of driving, which he's not fond of to begin with.

No doubt the simple thing would be to replace my car with his. Though I hate to admit it, I'm not quite ready to do that. But I do plan to replace my car as soon as technology is advanced enough to produce electric cars that are reliable for reasonable distances.

21. Sell the Damn Boat

∾

This suggestion is addressed to men. Women, for the most part, don't have these toys.

Fifteen million Americans own boats. Anyone who's ever been to a boating community on any weekend knows that only a very small percentage of these boats actually get used. Many are running up expenses in slips or storage lots around the country. The rest are taking up space in driveways or garages or the owner's backyard.

The same thing is true for many of the other sporting and recreational gadgets we Americans collectively have spent billions of dollars acquiring: downhill and cross-country skis, scuba gear, backpacks, fishing tackle, golf clubs, camping equipment, you name it.

If you've reached the point where you're beginning to doubt the bumper sticker that said "He who dies with the most toys, wins," maybe it's time to think about unloading some of them.

22. Build a Simple Wardrobe

This suggestion is, for the most part, addressed to women. Men already have simple wardrobes.

After years of trying to come to grips with the elusive concept of "fashion," I've come to one overwhelming conclusion:

When a man and a woman are together and comparably dressed in any style, from dressy to casual to unbelievably casual, almost without exception the man looks better than the woman. There are two reasons for this:

One: When it comes to fashion, men have it easy, and because of this they almost always get it right, and,

Two: Women have it difficult, and they almost always get it wrong. And some get it more wrong than others.

Let's face it, men have basically only four options: suit (with shirt and tie); slacks (with shirt and, sometimes, a jacket); casual pants, jeans (with polo shirt), or sweats; formal wear.

Women have unlimited options:

Suits, the jackets of which can be short, medium, long, or

very long; fitted, loose, boxy, or peplum; broad-shouldered, narrow-shouldered, drop-shouldered, or puff-shouldered; single-breasted, double-breasted, belted, or open, with collars, of every variety, or without collars; they can be round-necked, square-necked, scoop-necked, or V-necked; and are available in any fabric or combination of fabrics, and in any color or combination of colors imaginable.

Likewise, the options for the women's equivalent of the other categories—slacks and casual wear and formal wear—are also available in an infinite variety of styles, fabrics, and colors. This is the reason women have three times the amount of clothes in their closets as men do. They've got a dozen different fashion statements, and few, if any, of them work together.

My suggestion for creating a simple wardrobe is to take a lesson from the way men dress:

First, pick a simple, classic style that looks good on you, and then stick with it. Forever.

Second, build combinations of outfits that work as a *uniform:* Two or three jackets of the same or similar style but in different, muted shades, with two or three sets of the same or similarly styled skirts and/or slacks in different muted shades, and a couple of coordinating shirts/blouses/tops. *Each item should go with every other item.*

Third, remember that men, for the most part, don't wear jewelry (see #94), don't carry purses (see #93), and wear only one heel height (see #91).

This is not to say women should dress like men. But it's certainly possible to create a simple, functional, feminine wardrobe by following the same *principles* men follow when it comes to fashion.

23. Reduce Your
Go-Go Entertainment
∽

If you began your simplification program out of the need or the desire to cut back on your spending, your entertainment expenses were probably among the first to be reduced. If you're seeking simplicity as part of getting off the fast track, then reducing your need for outside entertainment will no doubt be high on your list. In either case, cutting back on your nightlife, and looking within yourself and to your family for entertainment, is a positive step toward simplification.

The financial rewards of avoiding such activities as movies, plays, theater, opera, concerts, cabaret, and nightclubs are obvious. The personal rewards may not be so apparent at first. After all, we've been compelled in recent years to go, to do, to be on the move, to experience all that money can buy. Oftentimes, in the process, the things we really *like* to do have been overlooked.

I was recently in a meeting with a dozen high-powered professional people. We started talking about our goals for our leisure time, and how seldom we allow ourselves to truly enjoy our own quiet moments. We each decided to make a list of the things we really liked to do.

The lists included things like:

Watching a sunset. Watching a sunrise. Taking a walk on the beach or through a park or along a mountain trail. Having a chat with a friend. Browsing in a bookstore. Reading a good book. Puttering in the garden. Taking a nap. Spending quiet time with our spouse. Spending quiet time with our children. Listening to a favorite piece of music. Watching a favorite movie. Spending time with our pets. Sitting quietly in a favorite chair and doing *nothing*.

We were surprised and delighted to see most of the things we listed required little or no money, no expensive equipment, and were available for anyone who wants to take advantage of them. For the most part, our favorite pleasures were the simple pleasures.

I don't pretend that this small group represents a major sampling. But as I travel around the country talking to people about simplifying their lives, I hear the same stories over and over again. People are tired of being driven by entertainment market forces. They're coming to realize the best things in life *are* free, and that doing less can mean having more—more serenity, more happiness, more peace of mind.

I urge you to make your own list of the things you and your family really love to do. And then arrange your life so that each day you have time to do as many of the things you like to do as possible.

24. Rethink Your Meals with Friends

⁓

One of the things Gibbs and I had to take a hard look at when we started to simplify was having people over for dinner. We enjoy spending an evening with special friends, but since meal preparation is not a high priority for either of us, we found the time and energy required to have even a casual dinner at home were more than we were willing to expend. Fortunately, after suffering through our home cooking, most of our friends agreed.

Now, we regularly meet friends at a local restaurant for a dutch-treat evening out. We avoid the shopping, preparation, cooking, and cleanup, and our time and energy have been freed so we can enjoy each others' company. It doesn't have to be expensive, and if you split an entree (#58), it doesn't have to be fattening. It doesn't even have to be an evening; Saturday and Sunday mornings are a great time to have a relaxing meal out with friends.

On the other hand, we know several people who've recently sworn off restaurant meals completely. They're tired of the expense, the noise, the secondhand smoke, and the lack of privacy at most restaurants. Like us, they're not all that fond of cooking, so, when they get together with friends, they've gone back to the potluck dinner where everyone can pitch in. They've instituted some new rules for that time-tested social gathering, however: people can bring whatever they like, as long as it's low in calories, moderate in quantity, and lacking in the competitive spirit.

25. Turn Off the TV

Studies have shown that in the typical American household the TV is on approximately seven hours per day. If you've been on the fast track these past years, the chances are good you haven't had a lot of time to spend in front of a TV. But you may be spending more time watching television than you realize. You may not have stopped to consider how your television viewing may be affecting you and your family, and how it's dictating your purchasing and life-style choices. I urge you to give some thought to it.

Think about whether the lives portrayed on your favorite sitcom contribute anything positive to your life, or whether repeated exposure to crime and violence contributes to your peace of mind. Think about whether the "thirty-second sound bite" format of most television news gives you any real information. Think about whether the addictive habit of watching television contributes to your aliveness, spontaneity, and sense of freedom.

And, if you've made the decision to reduce your need for

goods and services (#42), think about the overpowering effects of television advertising:

By far the largest percentage of the over $125 *billion* spent last year by advertisers was spent on television commercials. Christopher Lasch, in his best-selling book, *The Culture of Narcissism,* points out that modern advertising creates a consumer who is "perpetually unsatisfied, restless, anxious, and bored." Judging simply by the percentage of advertising dollars spent, it's reasonable to assume that television has done more to foster the consumer spending of the eighties, and what Lasch refers to as "the new forms of discontent peculiar to the modern age," than any other medium.

If you suspect the habit of watching television might be playing a significant role in the complexity of your life, I suggest you read *Unplugging the Plug-in Drug,* by Marie Winn. This book explains TV addiction, and offers an easy, step-by-step program both you and your children can use to reduce or eliminate the use of television.

Come up with a personalized list of things you can do, either by yourself or with your family, to take the place of watching TV, such as reading the classics again, or reading out loud from your favorite plays. Set up some board games or other types of games you can play with the family, such as charades, Twenty Questions, Monopoly, or Trivial Pursuit. Or, find a hobby that will consume you.

If you're addicted to television, kicking the habit will certainly simplify your life. People who've done it say it's one of the best things they've ever done.

26. Stop the Junk Mail

Americans receive close to two million tons of junk mail every year, half of which is never opened or read. For the half that is read, we spend an average of three or four days a year just *opening* it. One can only guess at the amount of time we spend each year reading unsolicited catalogs full of items we have no use for. What a waste. And what an annoyance. Especially if you are anything like a good friend of mine who feels guilty every time she receives a charitable fund-raising solicitation she doesn't respond to.

In addition to the personal nuisance junk mail creates, it also makes tremendous demands on our environment. If we stopped the unwanted junk mail we receive, we could save close to one hundred million trees every year.

Fortunately, there is something we can do to reduce the amount of junk mail that litters our mailbox each day.

First, write to Stop The Mail, P.O. Box 9008, Farmingdale, NY, 11735-9008. Request that your name and all variations of your name not be sold to mailing list companies. This will reduce your junk mail by up to 75 percent.

Second, whenever you request a catalog, ask that your name not be added to the mailing list. Or, if you want to receive that company's catalog but no others, request they not sell your name. Most legitimate companies will honor such a request.

Third, until you get your name removed from the mailing lists you don't want to be on, at the very least you can sort your mail over a waste basket or a recycling bin. Learn to be ruthless here. Rather than having to throw it out later, when the clutter has gotten out of hand, avoid the clutter process in the first place, and throw it out now.

If you could cut by even 50 percent the amount of mail you have to handle each day, wouldn't that simplify your life?

27. Cancel Your Magazine Subscriptions

∽

I have a friend who reads dozens of consumer magazines each month. She has an exciting and satisfying career, lives in a beautiful home, has two lovely and talented daughters, and they're all healthy. She has all these and many other reasons to be ecstatic. Yet she recently went through an extended period when she was consumed with the idea that she wasn't happy, and that her life just wasn't what it should be.

One day I happened to be looking through the stack of magazines on her desk. All of a sudden it hit me: One of the reasons she thought she was so unhappy was she was gauging her life by the unrealistic life-styles portrayed in these magazines.

Most consumer magazines are little more than vehicles for Madison Avenue. One of their primary purposes is to get us to buy the products they advertise. Month after month, year after year, they create expectations about our lives we're often not even aware of.

Indeed, with the possible exception of television, there are few places where the idea of unbridled consumption is more subliminal and more seductive than the advertising found in these magazines. Advertisers are now spending *billions* of dollars each year in print advertising. It's not surprising that, through the lure of page after page of enticing four-color ads, advertisers set our fashion and cooking and eating trends, and regulate and promote our social lives. They encourage us to smoke, drink and drive fast cars, and to buy expensive clothes, jewelry, furniture, and hundreds of other products that, for the most part, we don't really want, often can't afford, and which seldom live up to their advertising claims. Is there even a remote possibility, for example, that drinking Johnnie Walker Red will make a woman more appealing to a man?

You might want to consider how the magazines you read are affecting the way you spend your time and your money. If you can trace many of your buying patterns to your magazines, perhaps it's time to cancel your subscriptions. This is one of the easiest ways to reduce the number of "Buy! Buy! Buy!" messages you are exposed to every day and to free yourself from consumer addictions.

If you're a magazine addict, go cold turkey on this one. Find a new interest or hobby or reading program to fill in the time you used to spend poring over magazines. You might be amazed to see how much time you'll have to do the things you'd really like to do.

28. Stop the Newspaper Delivery

∞

We have good friends who have never been in the habit of reading the daily newspaper. He is a physicist; she is an artist. Until they recently purchased a VCR to watch their favorite movies, they never owned a TV. They've never watched the news on television. While most other people are reading the morning news, this couple is reading their favorite novels.

They keep up to date in their professions and with what is happening around the globe by reading professional journals. They feel they are each making a contribution to the world through their work, and do not feel obliged to meet other people's expectations with regard to being up on current events.

They are well educated, literate, interesting, vital people who long ago came to the conclusion that reading the daily newspaper did not contribute to their mental or emotional well-being, and they arranged their lives accordingly.

If you're tired of bad news, but can't face the thought of giving up your daily newspaper completely, you might consider giving it up for even a month or two. Having done it, I can tell you that taking a break from the news from time to time makes it easier to discriminate between the news I want or feel I need to know and the negative information that complicates my life without enhancing it.

Over and over again, when I first suggest to soon-to-be-former fast-trackers that they try eliminating the daily newspapers from their schedule, they are shocked by the very idea. But as they begin to experiment, especially if they've set up a satisfying replacement activity, they find breaking the newspaper habit is not as difficult as they first imagined. Cutting back on the negative input you're subjected to every day is a positive step toward simplifying your life.

If you're trying to reduce your need for goods and services, keep in mind that advertisers spend over $8 billion a year on newspaper advertising alone. Cutting back on your daily exposure to that level of consumer programming may be sufficient reason to stop the delivery of the daily newspaper.

29. Drop Call Waiting

I know not everyone will agree with me on this issue, but I can think of few "conveniences" of the modern phone age that are more irritating than the contrivance "call waiting." Not only is this system a rude form of interruption, but people who have it have to *pay for it.* And of course, if you have call waiting, the telephone company wants you to believe you also have to have—for a couple dollars more per month—the service known as "cancel call waiting"; and if you have that, you also have to have—for another couple dollars more per month—"priority call waiting."

Have we so lost touch with the art of communication that we can't just come directly out and say, "Excuse me, can I call you later? I'm expecting an important call now"? Or, perhaps more accurately, "Sorry, but there is someone else I'd rather be talking to." Are the phone calls we're receiving today so vital that we can't be satisfied with having just one call in progress, but we have to have two? Have our schedules gotten so out of control that we have to pay the phone company to keep us in line?

For small businesses that want to avoid the added expense of multiple phone lines, call waiting can perhaps be justified. But I can't believe that juggling two phone calls on the same line at the same time has ever made anyone's personal life simpler. If you agree, you can cancel this "service" and save approximately five dollars per month on your phone bill.

30. Don't Answer the Phone Just Because It's Ringing

I know there are people out there who are constitutionally incapable of letting a ringing telephone go unanswered. I am married to one of them. And I admit it took many years of almost constant telephone use to reach a point where I could harden my heart to a ringing phone. But now that I'm there, there's no going back.

It's a minor point in a simplification program, but just because it's convenient for someone to call you at this particular time does not necessarily mean it's convenient for you to answer. Just think of all the times a ringing phone has interrupted a sound sleep, a good soak in the tub, a hot meal, an interesting conversation, some important work, mad passionate sex, or simply a quiet evening of welcome solitude.

All I can say is thank goodness for the answering machine. Now it's at least possible to monitor your phone calls so that you can talk only to those you wish to talk to, when you wish to talk to them. If you don't have an answering machine, you can turn your phone off so you don't have to hear it ring when you don't want to be disturbed.

There's no question that the telephone is one of the greatest conveniences of the modern world. But it can be one of the greatest nuisances unless we learn to use it for our *own* convenience rather than someone else's.

31. Don't Answer the Doorbell, Either

~

There's something so importunate about a ringing doorbell. It's different from a ringing phone: whoever it is is *right there* on the other side of the door. I can't tell you how many times I've had a perfectly good meal ruined by a knock on the door. We've all been trained to be polite to guests, even uninvited ones. Often we think nothing of inconveniencing ourselves and other family members, letting our dinner get cold, for example, by answering a ringing doorbell to speak to someone we may not even want to see.

I've come to regard a ringing doorbell in the same way I do a ringing phone. Unless I have an appointment or am expecting a friend or a delivery, I simply don't answer the door if it's inconvenient. My friends know not to drop by without calling first.

"But what if it's the postman delivering a certified letter?" a friend asked me. Have you ever had *good* news by certified mail? As far as I'm concerned it can wait. "But it is so rude not to answer the door," she protested. Certainly we've been brought up to think that way. But I've come to feel that, in fact, it's rude for someone to show up at the door unannounced and expect me to drop whatever I'm doing and answer it just because it happens to be convenient for them.

I admit it does take some hardening of your social graces. But if you're regularly bothered by unannounced callers at your front door, learning to just let the doorbell ring can make your life a lot easier.

Or, consider installing a spyhole, so at the very least you know for whom you're opening your door and your time.

32. Get Rid of Your
Car Phone

$\wp$

You already know that I'm not fond of the sound of a ringing telephone, so please forgive me a certain level of prejudice on this issue.

I know many people who caved in when the price of car phones dropped below five hundred dollars. Some people, like the half-dozen real estate agents I know who have car phones and say they couldn't do business without them, presumably have a legitimate need to have constant access to a telephone. But most of the people I know, including even some of the real estate people, say car phones are another one of those "conveniences" that are more trouble than they're worth.

First, there's the safety factor, which has never been adequately addressed by the manufacturers, the regulatory agencies, or the media. More than one person I know has given up their car phone because of near-miss accidents that occurred when engaged in a heavy-duty conversation while barreling down the highway at sixty-five miles per hour. Worse yet are the clowns who are busy punching in a seven-digit phone number while maneuvering through rush-hour traffic with a five-speed stickshift car.

At the very least, use caution and common sense where you use a car phone. If you have to make a call en route, pull off to the side of the road to place your call. Or, if possible, have a fellow passenger make the call for you.

Second, there's the frustration of the as-yet-unperfected technology that causes conversations to fade in and out, or to be cut off altogether if you pass outside your calling area. This is convenience?

Third, safety aside, there is the sheer lunacy of committing ourselves to yet again doing at least two things at the same time. Have we really gotten *that* busy?

Fourth, there's the expense. If, as my father used to say, you've got more money than brains, there's probably no real harm done spending it frivolously on calls that could in most cases more easily and at far less expense be made from a stationary phone. But if you're working within a tight budget, you might want to seriously reconsider what having a car phone really saves you.

33.   If You Don't Like
the Holidays, Bow Out
୬

Major holidays are among the most stressful, and therefore least simple, times of the year. Be honest. How often have you fervently and possibly not so secretly wished that you didn't have to go through with today's commercialized Christmas and all the shopping, presents, cooking, office parties, family dinners, overeating, overdrinking, and overspending that's a long way from simple and in fact complicates your life a good deal?

I know there are people out there who actually love celebrating Christmas and all the other holidays. If you're one of them, that's great—do so, and enjoy. But if you can't bear the thought of sitting through another Christmas dinner, you're not alone. Studies show that for many people Christmas is the most depressing time of the year. Now that we're in the enlightened nineties, we know we all come from dysfunctional families. It's no big deal to finally admit that the holidays are a pain in the neck and move on to other things we'd rather do.

Imagine how you'd like to spend the time you've previously spent on holidays—ensconsed on the sofa with a stack of good books, relaxing in front of the VCR with your favorite movies, hiking, skiing, or even using the time for private reflection with your family—then set it up exactly as you'd like it to be. We know a couple with three teenage children who have forsaken the holidays altogether and go camping instead. It's a chance for closeness with each other and with nature and an opportunity to escape the commercialism they no longer want to have in their lives. We know another couple who decided years ago that Christmas was for children. They buy or make special Christmas gifts for the kids in their life, and make a donation to their favorite charity each year for the grown-ups.

To make the transition as easy and as painless as possible, announce well ahead of time to all your family and friends that you no longer want to do Christmas (or Thanksgiving, or Easter, or birthdays, or any one or all of these), or that you want to do it differently from now on and explain why. Let them know you'll be making other arrangements for the holidays.

Realize that not everyone is going to understand your position, and some might even be hurt by it. If the guilt becomes too heavy, you may have to compromise: Do Thanksgiving but not Christmas. Or whatever.

Also realize that while some may pretend to be hurt, they might actually be delighted that they don't have to suffer through another Christmas, but they're too tradition-bound to admit it.

Just think. If you act now, you can free yourself from one of the most stressful events of the year. Don't waste another moment. This year do Christmas your way.

34. Stop Sending
Christmas Cards

∽

"Stop sending Christmas cards? You've got to be kidding," moaned a friend of mine. "It's my favorite thing about Christmas."

If, like my friend, you love sending Christmas cards, by all means do it; this suggestion is not addressed to you. It is addressed to all those people who start grousing in mid-July that they haven't picked out their Christmas cards yet, and to all the ones who are still mumbling by the end of November that they haven't gotten around to addressing their cards yet, and to the ones who are still grumbling by the middle of December that they haven't had time to pick up the Christmas stamps from the post office yet, and they don't know how they'll possibly get them mailed in time for Christmas.

This is also addressed to those people who send printed-signature cards. Hand-picked or lovingly hand-produced Christmas cards are a joy to receive. What is surprising is that in these days of environmental awareness there are people and businesses that year in and year out are still sending the printed-signature, rubber-stamped, or signed-by-their-secretary Christmas cards. I've never been able to figure out what the message on these cards is, or why anyone would bother sending a card they didn't have the time to at least address, sign, and stamp themselves.

For many people, the printed-signature holiday card has become the symbol for what's wrong with Christmas. It's impersonal, it's commercial, it's expensive, the real message is not a positive one, it clutters up our lives, and it's an environmental waste.

If you're ready to stop sending Christmas cards, you can begin to let people know that this is your last year for doing cards. Or, cut your list by half or more and send cards only to those you truly want to keep in touch with. The chances are good the other people on your list will understand, and it may free them from feeling they have to send cards as well.

35.   Gift-Giving Simplified

I have a friend who has quite a large extended family and they all remember each other's birthdays and anniversaries, not to mention Christmas and other holidays, with gifts. Hardly a month goes by without my friend agonizing over what to give some member of her family whose birthday is approaching. Invariably, she ends up settling on something she is not happy with. Usually, neither is the recipient, though neither of them would ever admit it.

In trying to simplify the perennial problem of gift-giving, I've come to the conclusion that the Hobbits, in J.R.R. Tolkien's epic fantasy, were right: mathoms are the answer. A mathom was an object of any value for which a use could not be found, but which the owner was not prepared to discard completely. A Hobbit would never *buy* a gift; they gave mathoms instead.

When we started the uncluttering process of our simplification program (#1), I set up a section in our linen closet for items that would make good mathoms. It included things like vases, trays, decanters, little decorative bowls and boxes, toasters, a mini-Cuisinart, games we no longer used, and any extras I was getting rid of (#99) that might be appropriate.

I also announced to family and friends that from this day forward I'd be giving mathoms rather than buying presents. I figure if you're going to give someone you love something they probably have no use for, it should at least be blessed by having a history with you first.

Now, when special occasions arise at which a gift would be appropriate, I search in our closet for a suitable mathom. I've also let my friends know that they are free to pass on (or possibly fob off) these "treasures" to someone else whenever appropriate.

If you have the knack of gift-giving, please share it with those of us who don't. But if you find gift-buying an occasion for pulling out your hair, consider setting up a mathom box. Rather than spending untold hours shopping for and agonizing over gifts that are never quite right, you can go straight to your mathom box and find something that's absolutely not right.

And by the way, an excellent source for mathoms is all the gifts *you've* received over the years that have never been quite right either.

Don't forget to have your children set up a mathom box of their toys and games they no longer use. Have them get in the habit of thinking of other possibly younger children who would be delighted with a new-to-them toy. This creates a natural recycling process for your kids' toys, and is another lesson in uncluttering.

36. Traveling Simplified

Gibbs is, among other things, a travel writer. In the fifteen years we've been married we have traveled tens of thousands of miles all around the world. We've crossed huge oceans on tiny yachts; ridden trains across desolate continents; paddled up quiet waterways; rafted down whitewater rivers; hiked over scrub-covered mountains; and walked through many of the major capitals of the world.

If there is one thing we've learned in all these years, it's how to travel light, and still have everything we need. Well, almost everything.

The bind many travelers get into is, in addition to packing all the things they'll need for a two-week trip, they also pack all the things they *might* need for a two-week trip. Here are some ways to avoid that.

For most vacation travel, start by making a list of the different types of clothes you'd like to take, such as dressy, casual, sporty, and loungewear. Then cross off everything but the casual clothes. That's all you use for most trips.

Go to your closet and pull out all the appropriate casual clothes. (Now that you've simplified your wardrobe [#22], you won't have a lot of clothes to confuse you.) Fold them, and arrange them in piles on the bed, shirts in one stack, slacks in another, etc. Then put at least one half of the items from each stack back in your closet. Let's face it: if you get there and think you need something, in most cases you can get along without it. THIS IS THE SECRET TO TRAVELING LIGHT: THERE IS SO LITTLE WE REALLY NEED AND YOU CAN ALWAYS GET ALONG WITHOUT IT. (This is also the secret to simplifying your life.)

Wear and take only dark-colored clothes.

Make sure each piece of clothing you take can be worn with every other piece.

Always, even in hot climates, wear or take a blazer or jacket or vest with all the pockets you can get, and one that can go from casual to dressy, if need be.

Take only what will fit in one of the rollerboard-type cases with wheels. We recommend the TravelPro 727, available at most luggage stores. It's lighter in weight than the hard cases and holds more, though if an elephant sat on it, you'd have to get another one. Also, it has a plethora of outside pockets for conveniently stowing tickets, reading material, and other goodies, so you don't need any other bag. Best of all, it meets FAA regulations for carry-on luggage on all domestic flights and many, though not all, international flights.

Use a toilet kit or cosmetics bag that unfolds and can be hung on the back of a door or on a towel rack and that fits right into your TravelPro. (If you're a guy, you've probably already got a simple kit; if you're a woman, and have learned how to be drop-dead gorgeous in ten minutes [#90], you won't need a hair dryer, or any of that other stuff.)

Take only two pairs of shoes, both of the same height, preferably low-heeled, and both of them comfortable.

Imagine how simple it would be to take off for a month and go halfway around the world with only one small bag you can easily roll through busy traffic, up and down stairs, across railroad tracks, around grassy knolls, through cobbled streets, and over the Nullarbor Plain.

37. Take a Vacation at Home

∽

Some of the most fun and relaxing vacations Gibbs and I ever had we've taken at home. If you're just getting started on your simplification program, a vacation at home is a perfect way to begin.

You could start your vacation by getting rid of all the clutter in your life (#1). Making a family project out of this step is not only fun but a good way to set up a check system so that no one cheats.

Taking a vacation at home is also a good time to start a new hobby (#53), or to get your house in shape for speed cleaning (#3), or to plant a garden (#6), or to do any number of the things you've been wanting to do, but haven't had the time because you've been too busy and you're never home.

We spent one vacation getting to know our local community. We realized at one point that there were many visitors to our area who knew our town in some respects better than we did. So we took a day and went to all the art galleries and museums. We took another day and walked every street in the downtown area. We saw new stores and changes to old ones that we hadn't known about. We took another day and walked through several residential areas; we saw new houses and additions to old ones, and got a firsthand look at the local flora and fauna of our neighborhoods. We also had picnics on the beach and in a couple of our local parks. All of these things contributed to a new feeling of pride and familiarity with our town.

You could take a vacation at home to get caught up on your reading list. If you wanted to take a break from reading, you could watch new videos of favorite movies you've been wanting to see. A home vacation is an excellent time to organize a simple eating program (#57), to begin your daily exercise plan (#63), or set up the model ship building project you've been promising to do with the kids. Or, you could take a vacation at home and learn to do absolutely nothing (#82).

Hint: It's often easier if you tell your co-workers, friends, and especially your family that you'll be "away" on vacation. Otherwise, your vacation time may well be taken up by other people's crises.

Three

Your Finances

38. Get Out of Debt

There's a good chance that your parents, like mine, were survivors of the Great Depression. Throughout their lives my folks had one inviolate rule when it came to finances: If they didn't have the cash in hand, they didn't buy it. With the exception of the mortgage on their home, they never had a debt in their lives. They simply refused to take advantage of the post–World War II buy now–pay later mentality that has made us a nation of consumers and debtors. Whenever they needed a new piece of furniture or a major appliance, they took money from their "contingency" fund, or, if the fund was depleted, they *waited* until they had set the money aside by saving a little each month.

Many people from our parents' and our parents' parents' generation lived that way. Considering the fact that debt is one of the leading causes of emotional and psychological stress in our lives, many of us would do well to live that way today.

If you're one of the more than fifty million Americans for

whom credit card or installment debt has become a problem, there are a couple of things you can do:

1. *You can take steps to get out of debt on your own.*

This means sitting down and figuring out exactly how much you owe, then setting up a plan so that you can pay it off as quickly and as methodically as possible, even though it may take several years to do it. It also means making a promise to yourself to stay out of debt in the future. This solution is doable, but it requires discipline, determination, and a total commitment to getting out from under the stress caused by debt.

2. *If you suspect you're in over your head and you're beginning to think you'll never get out on your own, you can get help.*

Jerold Mundis, in his excellent book, *How to Get out of Debt, Stay out of Debt & Live Prosperously* (Bantam Books, available in paperback), offers a time-tested system for getting out of debt. Based on the principles used in Debtors Anonymous, the program he outlines has been used successfully for years to free thousands of people from a life of debt.

This solution also requires discipline, determination, and

commitment, but the book provides a proven, step-by-step program to help you along the way.

I can't promise you that getting out of debt will be easy, but it will certainly simplify your life.

39. Live on Half of What You Earn, and Save the Other Half

It's estimated that less than 10 percent of Americans are in the enviable position of having all their present and future financial needs taken care of. A large percentage of the people who will be retiring over the next twenty-five years will have little more than their Social Security payments to sustain them. And there aren't many people who are betting money that Social Security will be an adequate or even a viable source of retirement income in years to come.

We've become a nation of spenders rather than savers. While it's true that many people have been forced to live beyond their means because of the increase in the cost of living and the decline in the value of the dollar, it's also true that we spend far more than we need to on stuff we don't really require.

If you're feeling so out of control in terms of your spending that you think you couldn't possibly save a significant portion of your income, take a close look at *how* you spend your money. If you feel you can't make major cuts in your spending, start by cutting back by only 10 or 15 percent over the next year. Then cut back another 10 or 15 percent beyond that the following year, gradually building up to 50 percent.

Close to half of the items in this book will help you reduce your spending. Living simply is not a matter of living cheaply or of feeling deprived. On the contrary, it's an opportunity to get in touch with what is really important in your life, and to reach a level of moderation that will create not only a feeling of contentment and security, but also a sense of being in control.

If you've been living on the edge, getting to the point where you can stash away a good portion of your income each month to take care of your future needs will put you back in the driver's seat, and go a long way toward simplifying your life.

40. Rethink Your Buying Habits

Several years ago, Gibbs and I decided we needed to get a set of hand-held weights to use on our daily walks. So we rushed right down to the sporting goods store and spent fifty dollars on a set of Heavy Hands.

Over the next two weeks we used the set half a dozen times and then put them aside and never touched them again.

Six months later I gave the Heavy Hands to a friend who mentioned she was going to rush down to the sporting goods store to buy some hand-held weights. She has used them once and, if my guess is right, she'll never pick them up again, except possibly to pass them on to the next person she hears about who is going to rush down to the sporting goods store to buy a set of Heavy Hands.

This is just one example of the dozens of things we've bought over the years that we really didn't need and, after we'd used them for a short time, didn't even want. You no doubt have your own list of similar purchases, some more expensive than others, but all bought with the same compulsive "I've got to have this *now*" syndrome. For the average

American, our lives—and our homes, our cars, and our work spaces—are filled with the flotsam of our buying habits.

Once Gibbs and I could face the fact that we had yet again bought one more thing we didn't need, we decided we should rethink our buying habits. So we sat down and drew up a list of ways we could do things differently:

1. We designated one day a week for shopping; this includes groceries and anything else we think we might need.

2. Now, before we buy something, we think it through. Many of the things we buy are simply momentary gratifications. We've gotten into the habit of asking ourselves, "Do we *really* need this whatever-it-is?" "How *long* will we need it or want it?" "Will this be just one more thing to end up in the back of a closet?"

3. We delay all major purchases—and many of the minor ones—for at least two weeks, or even a month. We've found that by the time the end of the month rolls around we've figured out that we didn't really need the item, whatever it was, in the first place.

4. Or, alternatively, we see how long we can live without whatever it is we currently think we can't live without. Making a game out of this gives an extra boost to our determination *not* to acquire more clutter.

5. We try to come up with a creative solution rather than a buying solution to a perceived need. For example, there were many ordinary household items—books, or a pair of socks filled with sand—we could have used instead of running out to *buy* a set of Heavy Hands.

41. Change the Way You Shop

If you have trouble controlling the urge to buy, make it hard on yourself: go shopping if you must, but leave your cash, checkbook, and credit cards at home.

For many people, buying is nothing more than a habit. The way to break any habit is to replace the offending activity with another activity. Draw up a list of things you can do instead of shopping so that next time you get the urge to spend money on things you don't need, you'll have something else to do instead.

For example, take a walk, get together with a friend, go to the library, or take a cold shower—anything to avoid spending time shopping. Though initially you may feel deprived by the absence of shopping in your life, there is ultimately an exhilarating freedom in getting to a point where you don't *have* to buy.

Use the Buddy System. If there is something you've decided you absolutely must have, take a friend who is familiar with your buying habits and who is sympathetic to your desire to change them. Have your friend police your purchases so you buy only the item you set out to acquire. Make sure you pick the right buddy, though. I used to go shopping with a friend, and we'd spend time encouraging each other to buy things neither of us needed as a means to justify our own spending habits.

Pay for everything you buy by check. This makes it slightly more difficult than if you pay by cash or credit card, and also makes it easier to keep track of what you buy, and how you spend your money.

Practice looking at advertising with a jaundiced eye. It's the "thrill" of buying that is addictive. Once the thrill has worn off, you've got to do it again. That's what advertisers count on. Once you become aware of the control advertisers have over your money it's much easier to hold on to it.

42. Reduce Your Needs for Goods and Services

૭

One of the myths of the eighties was that the more goods we had and the more help we hired, the simpler our lives would become. In the process of simplifying I have found just the opposite is true.

Rethinking your buying habits (#40) and changing the way you shop (#41) will reduce the "goods" that clutter up your life. Many of the other steps outlined in this book will reduce your need for "services."

For example, once you start simplifying, your house will be so easy to take care of you won't need the cleaning lady; your meals will be so basic you won't need the cook; your errands will be so organized you won't need the chauffeur; your wardrobe will be so minimal you won't need a fashion consultant; your investments will be consolidated so you won't need a bookkeeper; your purchases will be limited so you won't need a shopping service; your entertainment will be reduced so you won't need a babysitter; your phone system so direct you won't need an answering service; your lawn will be eliminated so you won't need the gardener; your home will be uncluttered so you won't need a professional organizer; your relationships will be cleaned up so you won't need a psychotherapist; and your health and fitness program will be so easy you won't need a personal trainer.

Just the scheduling (not to mention the rescheduling), arranging for transportation, getting people to do things right, arranging to pay them, and finding someone to take their place when they quit (which they don't do until just about the time you've gotten them trained) is complicated enough to make me want to avoid most of these "services" like the plague.

Again, we're talking about personal choice here. We each have to decide for ourselves the point at which the goods and services we have in our lives cease to make our lives easier, and begin to become a burden. Our own goal was to arrange our lives so that we could easily take care of most of our personal needs and possessions on our own. We've created a whole new sense of freedom for ourselves by eliminating most of the goods and services we once thought we couldn't live without.

43. Get Rid of All But One or Two of Your Credit Cards

B<small>Y</small> the time we decided to simplify our lives, Gibbs and I between us had nine credit cards. We didn't *need* nine credit cards. We didn't *use* nine credit cards. We didn't even *want* nine credit cards. We had them because, like Everest to the climber, they were there. We could have had many more. They arrived, unbidden and with increasing frequency, in the mailbox. It was so easy to just add one more card to our system on the theory that you never know when you might need an extra one.

In fact, the only time we've ever used credit cards is for dining out and for traveling—and we always paid the bill in full each month. Not only were all these cards a nuisance to keep track of, but we had to pay anywhere from $25 to $100 a year for the "privilege" of carrying them.

It wasn't until I started reducing our junk mail (#26) that I began to realize that getting rid of all but one of our credit cards would be another step in simplifying our lives. Not only would it eliminate at least a dozen or more pieces of mail each month (in addition to regular statements, there are routine promotional pieces as well), but it would save us several hundred dollars a year in annual fees, as well as the hassle of carrying and rotating the cards.

After doing some research, we canceled all of our cards, and got one Visa card. We used one of the many banks that offer a choice of a $25 annual fee and an interest rate of 9 percent above prime on the unpaid balance, or no annual fee and a slightly higher interest rate. Since we pay off the balance each month, we chose the no annual fee. We now have a card that costs nothing and is very easy to keep track of.

It took us a while, but we finally figured out that having one or two credit cards is a convenience. Any more than that is more trouble than it's worth.

44. Consolidate Your Checking Accounts

❦

Early in our simplification program, I realized that my banking system had gotten out of hand. I had four or five separate bank accounts, which I had gradually been acquiring over the years: one for household expenses, one for business, one for contingencies, one for investments, one for savings. A banker friend told me that it's not at all uncommon for people to have multiple bank accounts these days; some at the same bank, some spread around banks all over town. Like many multiple account holders, I had deluded myself into thinking multiple accounts were a convenience.

In terms of the excess mail that multiple accounts generate, not only are there the regular monthly statements for each account, but there are all the additional monthly promotional pieces, credit card offerings, and other inducements that have to be sorted through with the real mail.

In terms of the banking, not only did each of those monthly statements have to be reconciled, but I had to keep track of four or five separate checkbooks in addition to having to keep track of which account was to be used for which expenditures.

More than once I had created major hassles for myself by writing checks on the wrong account.

Then, of course, there was the complication of making sure there were sufficient funds in each account to cover the checks.

If you find you are burdened by multiple checking accounts, getting rid of all but one of them will greatly simplify your banking chores. If you like the idea of keeping your savings fund and your contingency fund separate from your household funds—or whatever different accounts you have— you might want to consider adopting my simplified check register system outlined in #45.

45. Use This Simple Check Register System

ॐ

When I got rid of all but one of my checking accounts I still found it convenient to have separate categories for my expenditures, so I set up those categories in one account and used check registers to keep those categories separate.

For example, now I maintain three categories in my checking account: Household, Savings, and Investment. I use two standard wallet-sized check registers, fitted together on one side of my checkbook; on the other side I keep the checks.

Since I write more checks from the Household category, I label the first check register "Household." Then I divide the second check register into two categories, "Savings" and "Investments."

For ease in reconciling bank statements, I enter all my deposits in the "Household" section, and then "transfer" funds to the other sections, as needed. To do this, I simply make an entry in the "Household" section that reads "Transfer to Savings" and then list the amount, one thousand or whatever, in the debit column, and *deduct* that from the Household balance. Then I immediately turn to the "Savings" section, and make the appropriate entry, "From Household," and indicate the amount in the deposit column, which is then *added* to the balance in that section. If we decide to make a purchase with the money we have set aside in Savings, I simply record the check in the Savings section of the check register, and then deduct the amount from the total shown there.

It's the same with money shown in the Investment section. When we have built a sufficient investment balance, I write a check, say for a mutual fund purchase, and record the check in the Investment section of the check register, and deduct it accordingly.

When it comes time to reconcile a bank statement, I first sort the checks by category (Household, Savings, Investment), then go through each section of the check register and cross off the checks accordingly. Since all the bank deposits are shown in the Household section of the register, it's easy to confirm that each deposit is shown on the statement.

By maintaining these divisions internally in one account, I've eliminated all the other bank accounts, the other checkbooks, the other bank statements, and the need to reconcile them all. Obviously, you can set up any other categories that suit your personal needs. Just don't get carried away. Remember, the objective is to keep it simple.

46. Consolidate Your Investments

～

Over the past fifteen years or so, mutual funds have become the investment haven for small investors. I have a friend who woke up one day and realized she had funds in more than a dozen different mutual fund accounts. Actually, of course, she'd known all along that she had a number of different accounts, she just hadn't realized how much such diversity in her investments complicated her life. Dealing with the account statements and regular promotional mailings from each of the funds was a major headache, and tracking each of the accounts had finally become overwhelming. But it was the amount of time her accountant had to spend each year calculating the dividends and capital gains on all these accounts that was the nightmare.

Things had started out simply enough. When she started investing, she did some research, came up with a couple of funds she thought were good, and set up accounts in them. As time went on, she discovered other funds that sounded good, so she gradually started spreading out, both with her IRA funds and with her regular investments. Each time she heard of another stellar performance in a fund, she'd open another account.

Most investment advisers agree that as long as you pick a reputable family of funds, it almost doesn't matter which one you invest in over the long haul. The important thing is to set aside funds and invest consistently, year in and year out. If you want to diversify, say among income funds, growth funds, and tax-free funds, do so within the family of the fund you choose.

My friend has started gradually to consolidate her invest-ment funds. Her accountant has thanked her. Her mailman has thanked her. Even her trashman has noticed the lighter load.

47. Pay Off Your Mortgage

If you're living in the house of your dreams, you plan to stay there, and your mortgage payments are within your means, you might want to think about taking steps to pay down your mortgage early. Or pay it off entirely.

For years we've had it drummed into us that the tax savings of home ownership make carrying a mortgage worthwhile. You'll need to look at your own situation, and perhaps run it by your accountant, but when you do the numbers, the savings are actually not that significant. Besides, many people are beginning to realize that the freedom of owning their home outright far outweighs whatever tax savings there might be.

There are several ways you can approach mortgage pay-downs:

1. Lump sum payments. If, in addition to your regular salary, you receive sizable cash infusions from time to time, consider using them to pay down your mortgage. Before you make a large payment, however, make sure your lender will re-amortize your loan so that your monthly payments will be reduced.

2. Extra principal payments. You can significantly reduce the term of your mortgage and save many thousands of dollars over the life of your loan by making the next month's principal payment each time you make your regular monthly payment. You will need to get a copy of the amortization schedule from your lender. Or, if you have a variable rate loan, ask your lender for the calculation they use to figure the next month's principal payment.

3. Since the amount of the payment that is applied to principal increases with each payment, there may come a time down the road when the increased principal payment becomes more than you can handle. If that happens, you can simply pay whatever amount is comfortable for you toward the principal each month. You'll still save a substantial amount in interest payments, and be able to pay off your mortgage sooner than you would have otherwise.

4. Sell your home and move to a smaller, less expensive home. Depending on the equity you have in your home, and on real estate values in the area where you now live and in the area you would be moving to, it is possible you could use the proceeds from the sale of your current home to pay for your

new home in full, or at least significantly lower the amount of the new mortgage. Again, you'll want to check with your accountant. If you're approaching age fifty-five, keep in mind your $125,000 tax exclusion.

Any of these mortgage paydown plans assume that you have paid off all other outstanding debts, such as credit cards or installment loans, and that you have sufficient funds set aside for emergencies and investments. Paying your mortgage early will not necessarily *immediately* simplify your life; but it will get you out from under the eternal psychological pressure of monthly mortgage payments.

48. Next Time You Buy a Car, Get It Secondhand

When you consider that a new car loses 30 percent or more of its value the moment you drive it off the sales lot, you have to wonder why anyone would ever purchase a brand-new car.

A high percentage of new-car buyers trade in their cars every two to three years. These trade-ins are an excellent source of used cars. Often, they've been carefully driven and diligently maintained, so it's relatively easy to pay a mechanic to determine if there are any major defects. Generally speaking, if a car is going to develop problems, it'll happen in the first ten to fifteen thousand miles.

Also, keep in mind that after two years, a car has dropped another 30 percent from its original value. So, if you buy directly from the owner—never from a used car dealer—you can save 60 percent off the original sticker price of the car.

Not only will buying a secondhand car save you money and, one hopes, the hassle of financing and monthly payments, but, if you buy carefully, you'll have a car that has already had the bugs worked out of it, and that you can probably count on for many thousands of miles of trouble-free driving.

49. Teach Your Kids Fiscal Responsibility

I have a friend who recently found herself in reduced circumstances because of a divorce. As part of the divorce settlement she agreed to give up her high-powered foreign car, and to buy a somewhat more modest set of wheels. She took her ten-year-old son with her to pick out the new car and ended up, at her son's importunate urging, buying the most expensive model with leather seats, pinstriping, and, for an additional fifteen hundred dollars, gold trim. She was lamenting that she had spent all this extra money because she hadn't been able to tell her son that she couldn't afford it.

We all want the best for our children, and certainly there are times when it's hard to say no. But I can't help but wonder what kind of lessons we are teaching our kids by spending money on glitz and glitter "image builders," especially when we can't afford them.

As we are forging new spending habits for ourselves, either by desire or necessity or both, we should also be building sensible buying habits for our kids. Children are adaptable, and can learn to adjust quite well to a reasonable set of limits.

We just have to make sure they know what the limits are.

Teach your kids to save half of what they earn from their allowance or parttime jobs. Kids can learn, just as we are learning, that we don't have to have everything we see or everything the Joneses have. Kids can learn, just as we are learning, that there are options: if they get the gold trim on the car they can't have the new dirt bike. Kids can learn how to budget so their expenses don't exceed their income. Kids can learn, as we are learning, how advertisers appeal to our emotions rather than our needs. Kids can learn that if they don't have the money, they can't afford it, and that buying on credit can often lead to serious financial difficulties.

Teaching our kids how to handle their money is one of the most powerful gifts we can give them. And not only will it ultimately simplify their lives, but it'll simplify our lives, too.

Four

Your Job

50. Stop Being a Slave to Your Day Runner

∽

I first started making "to-do" lists when I was in the third grade. Over the years, I graduated from simple 3″ × 5″ spiral notebooks to an 11″ × 16″ black leather briefcase-type three-ring-binder time-management system with a two-page spread for my daily schedule and up to a dozen tabulated sections for goals, priorities, strategies, decisions, communications, addresses and phone numbers, forward planners, backward planners, mind maps, expense summaries, personal information, daily (and monthly and weekly and yearly) calendars, and a priority management overflow chart (whatever that was). Any yuppie worth his salt is familiar with this or a similar system for personal organization.

I actually spent a day and a half and more dollars than I'm comfortable admitting learning how to use this organizer. It required a commitment of at least thirty minutes each day to evaluate progress, check off completed items, and transfer unfinished business to the next day's two-page spread. Fully loaded, the binder weighs over five pounds, occupies 4.2 square feet of desk space, and I couldn't go around the block without having to lug it with me in case I was overcome with a brilliant idea, or remembered something I had to add to my Communication Planner Sheet.

For some people, these organizers probably serve a useful function (in addition to making money for their franchisers). I made zillions of phone calls each day, scheduled appointments around the clock, had a handful of projects going at any one time, and definitely needed a way to keep track of it all. It was just that, like many other yuppie Type A personalities, I'd overdone it.

Fortunately, I looked at my planner one day and realized I didn't want my life to be that complicated. This was the beginning of my simplification program.

Gradually, over time, I simplified not only my home and personal and business life, but my planning system as well. I went from that gargantuan book to a 3″ × 5″ appointment calendar, which can fit into a small pocket, but stays on a tiny corner of my desk most of the time. There were several stops in between, but I finally reached a size and a system that was compatible with my simple life.

If you're controlled by your time-management system, maybe it's time to look at how you can change it so that you control it instead.

51. Work Where You Live or Live Where You Work

࿔

A few years ago Gibbs worked in a major metropolitan area and we lived in the suburbs, nearly two hours away by commuter train. This meant that he, like millions of other commuters, often spent more than four hours each day just getting to and from his office. Usually, he'd leave the house at 6:30 in the morning and return home around 7:00 in the evening. Is this madness? Yes. Why do we do this to ourselves? For many people it comes under the category of "getting ahead." We finally faced the fact that we were trading our present for a questionable future. So we made some major changes in our lives.

We moved to a part of the country where we could live in the same town where we worked. What a difference. Now we can linger over breakfast in the morning after we've taken our brisk three-mile walk along the beach. Gibbs leaves the house around 8:15 and arrives at his office before 8:30. At least once a week he takes off early on a Wednesday afternoon and spends several hours climbing to the top of our local mountain peak to clear his head. He's always home by 5:30 in the evening, and when the days are long we frequently go for a paddle, or perhaps take another walk before dinner. Maybe we'll spend some quiet time together reading, or watching a beautiful sunset; things that are important to us, and which we could never do when he was trapped on a steamy, smelly, overcrowded, frequently late, and always uncomfortable commuter train. These things are also hard to do when one is stranded in commuter traffic on the freeway.

Yes, we no doubt gave up some career "advancement" by moving away from the hub, but the vast improvement in the quality of our lives more than makes up for it. The only thing we wonder is why we didn't make the move sooner.

52. Do What You Really Want to Do

୬

Few things complicate your life more than spending eight to ten hours a day, five to six days a week at a job you don't like, doing something you don't want to do.

Unfortunately, the *process* of figuring out what you want to do and then doing it isn't necessarily simple. Unlike canceling your newspaper subscription (#28), which can be completed with a phone call, setting up your life so that you're doing what you really want to do can take months.

Your task will be easier if you know what you want to do. Simply make up your mind to make the switch, and then do it. The process will no doubt include research, making new contacts, updating your résumé, possibly going back to school, maybe making a move across town or across country, and in some cases starting all over again.

If you don't know what you want to do, you have the added burden of figuring it out, which could mean research, testing, counseling, experimentation, and then, as above, figuring out *how* to do it, including most likely starting all over again. But having just spent two years figuring out what it is I want to do, and then arranging my life so I can do it, I can promise you it will be worth whatever complications you have to go through to get there, and it will definitely simplify your life in the long run.

53.   Turn Your Hobby
Into Your Job

Ｏne of the wonderful benefits of simplifying my life is that I have created more time to devote to my hobby, reading. But it can work the other way, too—making time for your favorite pastime can simplify your life.

A few years ago my friend Sandra, an attorney, took a leave of absence for the entire summer to visit her sister, who lives in Italy. They were in a small village in the mountains with not a whole lot going on. Her sister suggested they visit a neighbor's sculpting studio. Sandra knew nothing at all about sculpture and wasn't really interested, but because there was nothing else to do, she agreed to go along. She didn't know it then, but she'd found a hobby that would eventually change her life.

She spent every day for the rest of her vacation in that studio, learning everything she could about sculpting. When she returned home, she enrolled in a sculpture class. She resumed her legal practice during her workday, but her evenings and weekends were now devoted to her stone. Gradually, she began to acquire the various tools she needed, and, eventually, she set up a studio in her home. Before long she was selling her work at local art shows. Recently, she resigned from her law practice and is now a full-time sculptor. She exhibits her work regularly at galleries around the country.

Sandra says her life has never been better—or simpler. Before sculpting, her life was filled with phone calls, appointments, depositions, briefs, court appearances, and the endless number of other things required by the legal profession. Now, her life consists of getting up in the morning, pulling on her jeans, and going to her studio to sculpt. Her gallery manager handles all the mundane details of her business. Of course, the fact that she is doing something she truly loves also contributes to the simplicity in her life.

I have another friend who combined his hobby, helicopter flying, with his profession, physical therapy. He set up his new business in a remote resort area where there is a lot of hiking and other physical activities and, consequently, vacationers with physical injuries who need to be flown out to medical facilities. He simplified his life so he could do what he wanted to do, and his life has never been busier or more complicated. But it's a complication he loves, and that makes all the difference in the world.

In any case, if you're not already doing what you love, starting with a hobby is one way to get there.

54. Work Less and
Enjoy It More

～

Once I decided to simplify my life, one of the first things I did in terms of my business life was to cut back on my workday by 10 percent. I simply scheduled my day to end an hour earlier. I was surprised at how easy it was, and how little difference one hour less made in terms of my productivity. In fact, if anything, my productivity increased. Gradually, I cut back another hour or so, with little loss in production and a great increase in satisfaction. As I began to look at why this was so, I found that I had fallen into the trap of believing that I had to do everything today, or at the very latest, by tomorrow, so I was constantly working under unnecessary pressure, which is no fun.

Bit by bit, I learned to prioritize phone calls. Not *every* call had to be returned immediately. Some could wait a day or two; some could wait a week even. I found, to my delight, some never had to be returned at all.

In terms of projects, I learned to set up more realistic time-frames in which they could be completed, and began to realize, as with the phone calls, not everything had to be done today. I started doubling the time I estimated a particular project would take for completion. Not only was it easier to finish things on time, but there was less stress involved because I wasn't struggling to meet an impossible deadline.

I decided to build time into my schedule—at least an hour each day—for interruptions such as phone calls, unplanned meetings, searching for misplaced papers, and other time-robbers that are unavoidable in today's business world, but that we seldom account for. This meant even another hour of "unproductive" time, but these interruptions had always been there. Scheduling them simply forced me to admit they existed, and reduced the consequent anxiety about them.

Admittedly, because I was working for myself, I didn't have a boss breathing down my neck. But at the same time, anyone who has done it knows that we often create much more unrealistic schedules for ourselves than any boss ever would.

Whether you've been working ten- and twelve-hour days for yourself or for someone else, working less—even if you start by cutting back an hour or two only one or two days a week—is a realistic and effective way to get more out of your workday.

55. Stop the Busy Work

Busy work is the nonproductive time we spend sharpening pencils, cleaning out our desks, making unnecessary phone calls, getting another cup of coffee, organizing our schedule, drawing up reports, doing research, making more unnecessary phone calls—things we convince ourselves have to be done before we can get down to our real work. Some busy work is unavoidable and necessary. What I'm talking about here is the avoidable kind.

There are two reasons for busy work. One, we don't want to do what we're really supposed to be doing. Two, we don't have anything that has to be done, but we want to look busy. In this age of workaholism, busy work has been elevated to an art form. It is the phenomenon that in many cases makes it seem imperative that we spend ten to twelve hours a day in the office.

One of the first things I gave up when I started working less but enjoying it more (#54) was busy work. It's difficult to define exactly what that would be for you, since the actual activities vary from person to person, and from job to job. But at some level you know if you're doing it, even though you probably wouldn't want to have to admit it publicly. I can only tell you that when you stop the busy work it'll simplify your life, not because you'll be doing less, but because a greater percentage of your work time will, I hope, be spent doing work that is much more satisfying. If you prioritize before you start work, and then don't do *anything* unless it's on your list, a lot of busy work will just evaporate.

56. Include Your Family in Your Work Life

I have a friend who is a successful television producer. She works long hours in her office and on the set and is very good at what she does. She is married to a freelance artist who works at home and is Mr. Mom to their two young children.

One of the things Catherine and Jack decided to do to simplify their family life was to involve their children in their work life. The children are familiar with their father's work, since they're free to come and go in his art studio at home, and they've been to the galleries where his work is sold. At least two afternoons a week Jack takes the children to Catherine's office for lunch, and then to spend an hour or so on the set, watching their mother at work. They've met all of Catherine's co-workers, and most of their families, since Catherine encourages her staff to bring their children into the studio as well.

While having two young children in her office during her workday has been time-consuming for both parents, Jack and Catherine feel it's well worth the effort. The children have a good understanding of what their parents do when they are away from them, and they feel connected with work-related conversations between the parents. Before Catherine started involving the children in her work, they cried furiously when she left for the office and hated her leaving. Now that they know where their mother is going, the people she will be spending her time with, and approximately what she will be doing, they're much more amenable to her daily departure for the office.

An added and, at least to Catherine, unexpected benefit of having young children in the workplace on a regular basis has been that it helps to relieve the stress of a hectic and demanding job environment. Many of her harried executives have found it's a special treat to be able to walk into the office and spend even a few moments holding a laughing, bouncy baby, or to take the time to explain a procedure to a wide-eyed curious child. Having the children around has brought the staff closer together, too, since they have had an opportunity to get to know the special talents and needs of the other family members.

Obviously, not every workplace is set up for visiting children. But it might be worthwhile to think about ways you could involve your children in your work life. Perhaps you can take them to the office on the weekend, when things are less hectic. Have them meet your co-workers and, if possible, their children. Explain to them what it is you do, and show them samples of your work, or the results of your work. Keeping families together is certainly one way to relieve the complexity of today's world. Involving your children in your work life is a good way to start.

F i v e

Your Health

57. Simplify Your Eating Habits

~

It's only fair to confess that my idea of gourmet cooking is slicing a peanut butter and jelly sandwich on the diagonal. I realize my opinions about simple eating habits may not appeal to the gourmets out there—but once we started to simplify, I decided to cut, by at least half, the time I spent in the kitchen cooking. Now, it's ten minutes, max, from fridge to table. (I mean, why should I spend a lot of time cooking when our favorite meal in all the world is a bag of blue corn tortilla chips with fresh guacamole?)

In addition to cutting our meal preparation time in half, I had two other objectives when it came to simplifying our eating habits:

One, even though at heart I really am a junk-food junkie, I wanted our diet to be healthy and nutritious. To us that meant primarily fresh fruits and vegetables and grains.

Two, I wanted it to be low in calories, fat, and cholesterol. Again, that meant fresh fruits and vegetables, in as close to their natural state as possible—no whipped, frothy, sugary concoctions for the fruit, and no cheese sauces or gravies for the veggies. It also meant cutting back on meats, especially red meats.

Also, I wanted to eliminate processed foods from our diet entirely.

Now, our meals look something like this:

Breakfast: fresh squeezed orange juice or fruit in season, and homemade granolas, or fresh homemade oat bran muffins. (For a simple recipe for delicious fresh fruit muffins see #61.)

Lunch: Fresh fruit and/or vegetable crudités, with whole-grain bread sandwiches, such as sliced roasted turkey or avocado, tomato, and sprouts.

Dinner: Huge fresh salad or cold soup, such as gazpacho in summer; or hearty veggie soup and salad in winter; or steamed veggies with rice dishes.

There are no surprises here. This is basically the diet food and health specialists have been recommending for years. The real surprise to us was that in simplifying our diet in this way, not only did we cut our meal preparation time in half, we also cut our monthly food bill by more than half. I'm constantly amazed, as I go through the grocery store with our computerized shopping list (#4), at all the things we *don't* buy. And now that we've come close to eliminating packaged foods from our diet, we have greatly reduced the amount of trash we have to dispose of each week.

58.   Always Split a Restaurant Meal

When Gibbs and I were first married, we thought nothing of going out for a restaurant meal once or twice a week. We'd each order an appetizer with our before-dinner drink, then we'd scarf down the fresh baked bread (slathered with butter, of course) while waiting for our salads and the first bottle of wine. We'd each order an entrée, such as steak, veggies, and baked potato (with butter *and* sour cream). Then we'd finish off the dinner with a 1,000-calorie dessert and an after-dinner liqueur. Boy, are those days gone forever.

Gradually, the numbers on the scales began to get higher and higher, and we realized we'd have to make some changes. It took some experimentation, but we've finally over the years developed a system that works for us:

Both of us have stopped drinking alcohol; we got tired of the fuzzy head the morning after, and we'd rather save the calories for dessert. We've learned (reluctantly) to ask the waiter to remove the basket of fresh baked bread and the butter. Now, we split the entrée or, if we can't both agree on the same one, we each order an hors d'oeuvre. This, with a salad, is usually more than enough for one person, especially when we have a dessert—split, of course.

It is the rare restaurant that has learned how to serve reasonably sized portions for people who are concerned about their health and weight. Even rarer is the restaurant that takes into account the fact that, generally speaking, women need smaller portions than men. I know few clean-plate clubbers who, when faced with a heaping plate of what might be their favorite dish, can resist eating every single bite. And besides, there are all those starving children in China.

These days, most restaurants will allow you to split an entrée. Even if they charge a "split fee," it's well worth paying when you consider that if you order a whole entrée, and eat only half of it, the other half goes to waste; if you eat the whole entrée, it goes to your waist. If you find yourself in a restaurant that either doesn't serve human-sized portions or that won't split, don't patronize it and let the management know why.

We love eating out from time to time. Splitting a meal makes it possible for us to do so without the guilt and the distress of overeating.

59. Have a Fruit or Juice Fast One Day a Week

⌒

Another way to simplify your eating habits is to have only fresh fruit or fresh fruit juices one day a week.

I did this for years when I was single. I picked Saturdays because that was then the least demanding day of my week. I was usually at home, where I had easy access to the blender, and I could create the feeling of a "spa" weekend by relaxing and taking it easy.

After I got married, I switched my fruit day to Monday. Not only had the nature of my weekend changed, with a husband and an instant family, but eating only fruit on Monday seemed like a proper balance to the excesses of what was developing into our weekend pattern. Having nothing but fresh fruit one day a week certainly was a help in maintaining our weight.

Now that we've simplified our eating habits, we still have all-fruit days on a regular basis. One of our favorite treats is a drink made from an apple, a banana, a couple of oranges, and a handful of fresh strawberries or blueberries, or maybe a fresh peach. Obviously, any fresh fruit of your choice would work. We toss everything into the blender and press the button. It makes a fresh frappé that is a filling meal by itself. It's so good it almost feels sinful, and it couldn't be simpler.

60. Make Water Your Drink of Choice

‿

The most widely consumed liquids, in the order of preference, are coffee, sodas, diet sodas, milk, alcoholic beverages, carbonated fruit drinks, and teas.

There are many reasons to make water your drink of choice, but perhaps the best reason is that very few of the alternative liquids are good for you.

We're all familiar by now with the many and varied problems associated with each of these liquid refreshments, not the least of which are the empty calories or the potentially harmful additives in sodas and sugar-free drinks. I switched to drinking water almost exclusively years ago when I realized that the alternatives were highly caloric. It was a personal choice; I decided I'd rather save my calories for something like chocolate mousse.

If you did nothing more than substitute water for these liquids in your diet, you could easily lose ten to fifteen pounds over the next year. If you fall into the over 75 percent of the population that is at least 20 percent overweight, that may be reason enough to switch to water.

If your local tap water is good and clean, there is probably no need to buy bottled water. The tap water in our area tastes terrible so we drink bottled water, which, compared to any of the other liquids mentioned above, is inexpensive and readily available. With ice and a slice of lemon, we find it preferable to designer waters like Perrier and Calistoga.

If you're used to drinking highly flavored or stimulating liquids, water may seem boring at first. But after drinking water for a change, you'll wonder how you ever drank some of those yucky-sweet sodas and carbonated or caffeinated beverages we as a nation have become addicted to. Also, you'll be amazed at the reduction of glass and aluminum cans you have to worry about recycling.

Certainly if you have kids, one of the biggest favors you can do them is to keep them away from carbonated sodas. Someday they'll thank you.

Hint: Remember, coffee and caffeinated and carbonated drinks are addictive, so you'll need to brace yourself for the physical and psychological hazards accordingly. Even if you're not a heavy coffee drinker, quitting cold turkey can sometimes cause severe withdrawal symptoms, including migraine headaches, depression, and nausea. Start by cutting back by half for the first week, then by a quarter the second week. By the third week you should be able to quit altogether without adverse effects.

61. Eat a Muffin

∽

Several years ago, after routine blood tests, both Gibbs and I found we had elevated cholesterol levels. After doing some research, we decided to significantly reduce our consumption of red meat. And, we got on the oat bran wagon.

We replaced our weekend eggs-and-bacon breakfasts with blueberry oat bran pancakes and maple syrup (but no butter). Also, Gibbs started experimenting with oat bran muffin recipes, and ultimately developed his own delicious, low-fat version, shown below. We started eating oat bran muffins in place of breads. Within a few months we had lowered our cholesterol levels to within acceptable ranges and, as an added benefit, we both lost weight. .

Every week or so we make up a double batch of muffins—about two dozen. With all the ingredients on hand it takes roughly ten minutes to mix the batter, and another fifteen minutes or so to bake them. (This exceeds my ten-minute rule [#57] but, since it makes a two-week supply, I can justify it.)

These muffins are great with fruit or cereal for breakfast, with salads or soups for lunch, as a low-calorie, high-fiber between-meal snack, or even to keep the wolves from the door at bedtime. They're so delicious it seems amazing that they are also good for you. We expect to hear any day now that the cholesterol scare was a hoax, and that oat bran causes dancing deliriums in mice, or some such thing. In the meantime we continue to enjoy this simple, healthy treat.

Gibbs's Oat Bran Muffins

2¼ cups of oat bran (not bran flakes)
1 tbsp baking powder
¼ cup sugar or maple syrup
2 tbsp chopped almonds
handful of raisins or blueberries
¼ cup shredded coconut (optional)
1¼ cup nonfat milk
whites of two eggs, or one large egg if you're not concerned about cholesterol
2 large overripe bananas

Combine all dry ingredients in a mixing bowl. Blend all other ingredients into a puree and mix thoroughly with the dry ingredients.

Fill muffin tins, allowing some room for mix to rise. If you use blueberries, it's easier if you add them by hand to the filled muffin tin.

Bake at 450°F until top of muffins are brown (about 15 minutes). Makes approximately one dozen muffins.

As soon as they're cool, we bag them and put them in the freezer. Whenever we want one, we pop it in the microwave oven for 30 seconds on high.

62. Pack Your Own Lunch

∽

This idea came about as a measure of self-defense against business lunches and the "I'll just grab a quick bite" method of solving the perennial question of what to do for lunch.

If, like me, you love to eat and tend to go overboard when ordering food in a restaurant, there is only one solution to business lunches: don't do them. This may put a crimp in your business style—though there are alternatives—but it will do wonders for your waistline and your budget.

(The alternatives to business lunches are business breakfasts—where you can get by with ordering fresh orange juice or a slice of melon, or a "Let's do Perrier" mid-afternoon or before-dinner meeting. The other alternative is to practice moderation when ordering from a menu, but since I have so little self-discipline when it comes to food, I don't know how to tell you how to do that.)

Packing your own lunch offers several advantages over eating in restaurants, or grabbing a quick bite. First, you have control over what you eat. You can pack your own fresh fruits or vegetables or sandwich makings, and not have to worry about being at the mercy of the empty-calorie, highly processed foods of most food vendors.

Second, you can control the amount you eat. How often have you been overwhelmed by the sheer quantity of food on the plate a waiter puts in front of you? And how many times have you eaten it all because a doggie bag wasn't feasible, and you couldn't stand to let it go to waste? Just make sure you pack your lunch *after* you have your breakfast, when you're not feeling hungry.

Third, there's no question that packing your lunch is less expensive than restaurant or food vendor meals.

You might argue that packing your own lunch is just one more thing to add to the list of things you have to do each day. But if you plan for it on your computerized shopping list (#4), and get into the routine of it, the actual preparation time is minimal. Any way you slice it, making your own lunch has to take less time than it takes to get to a restaurant, stand in line for a table, place your order, wait for it to arrive, eat it, wait for the bill, argue with your luncheon date about who's going to pay for it, calculate the tip, pay the bill, wait for the receipt, and make your way back to the office.

When you're planning what to pack in your lunch, don't forget an apple. The apple is almost a perfect food. Not only is it full of vitamin C and other vitamins, minerals, and nutrients your body needs, it's also high in fiber and has no fat. The pectin in apples can soothe overstressed stomachs, and it's a passable substitute for after-meal brushing. An apple or even two for lunch on Monday is an excellent antidote to a weekend of overeating. Besides all this, the apple comes in its own packaging, travels well, and keeps indefinitely. What could be simpler?

63. Beware Exercise Equipment,
Fire Your Personal Trainer,
and Go Take a Walk

∽

There's a wonderful scene in the movie *Alice* where a fashionable yuppie has to reschedule her appointment with her personal trainer, who can't come for his appointment until after her session with her Rolfer, which has to be rescheduled so she can meet with her chiropractor. After that, she can go to the club for her massage and shiatsu lessons, which she plans to do following her Nautilus routine, but before the Swede walks on her back.

This is only a slight exaggeration of the rigorous physical exercise regimen many of us have set up for ourselves. Does all this go-go exercise do us any good? It might if we stuck with it, but the road to flab is paved with good intentions. The average number of times a new exercycle is used is 7.2, then it either sits in the corner of the room, cluttering up your life and making you feel guilty, or it goes into the next garage sale. Every day this expensive equipment—or the health club membership—goes unused, the guilt level rises, which only increases the stress in our lives.

We've become so addicted to compulsive, competitive behavior that we've even extended it to exercise, which, theoretically, we do for relaxation, and to improve and maintain our health. Now is the perfect time to get off the high-tech equipment sports treadmill and go take a walk.

Walking requires no fancy equipment, no new clothes, no club membership, and it's the best exercise you can get. Studies at the National Institute of Health and the Department of Physical Education of the U.S. Marines have shown beyond question that a thirty-minute walk every day, or even only three times a week, provides all the aerobic exercise anyone needs to maintain good health. Not only does a good, brisk walk energize the heart and lungs and respiratory system, but it clears the head and soothes the soul. It provides an excellent opportunity to get in touch with nature every day, to listen to the birds, to savor the seasons, to give a friendly nod to neighbors, to walk your dog, or to have a quiet few moments on your own just to treasure and enjoy.

Try it for one month. Get up half an hour earlier and go for a walk, in good weather or bad. If you don't like to walk alone, set up a buddy system with your mate or a good friend. Or have your kids join you on your daily walks. This is a good way to teach your children the importance of regular exercise. Once you've done it for a month, commit to it for six months.

After you've walked regularly for six months, the chances are good you'll stick with it for life.

There are few things you can do that will be better for your soul, and nothing you can do that will be easier, less stressful, and more beneficial for your body.

64. Get Up an Hour Earlier

The best hour of the day is the hour just before the time you are currently getting up. If you're like most people, you schedule your wake-up hour so that you have just enough time to get dressed, grab a bite of breakfast, take a quick peek at the headlines or the morning news, maybe help get the kids off to school, and get to work by eight-thirty or nine o'clock. There's not much time in there for lollygagging.

Imagine how nice it would be if you had a whole extra hour in the morning to do some things you've been wanting to do, like taking a walk (#63), or establishing your own morning ritual (#67), or just to have enough time for a leisurely breakfast with your family.

Adding an extra hour to your day, especially if you use it to do something other than work, is a very effective way to relieve stress and to give yourself the feeling of having much more time throughout the day. Studies have shown that we need less sleep as we advance in years. It could be that extra hour in the morning would do you a lot more good if you were awake and enjoying it, rather than trying to catch up on sleep you don't really need.

If you've never had an opportunity to enjoy that quiet hour before dawn, I urge you to start doing so tomorrow. You'll be amazed at the richness, peace, and simplicity it can add to your life.

65. Be in Bed by Nine
One Night a Week

A friend suggested this idea to me several years ago. It appealed to me immensely, and Gibbs and I incorporated it into our simplicity program. We made Friday night our night to be in bed by nine. Not only does it provide a satisfying end to a busy work week, but it gives us a head start on having a relaxing weekend. We find ourselves looking forward all week to our quiet, early-to-bed Friday evening.

If you've cut back on your go-go entertainment (#23), you may be staying home on Friday night anyway, so this would be a good night to start with. Sunday is also a good night for being in bed by nine, since there is usually so little happening on Sunday evenings, and the extra sleep could give you a good jump start on your busy week ahead.

Whatever night you choose, this investment in your sleep will provide you with an excellent return. You'll be more refreshed than on nights when you stay up late, and the added energy will make you more efficient at work and at play.

Since I secretly love to sleep, it took me a while to figure out why I hadn't thought of this on my own. It finally dawned on me that, because I have a heavy dose of the Protestant work ethic, I felt there was something almost decadent about going to bed early unless I wasn't feeling well. Many former yuppies I've talked to have had that same reaction.

But there is an amazing thing that happens when you begin to simplify your life: A lot of those once valued but often restricting beliefs—like the Protestant work ethic, idle hands are the devil's workshop, don't put off till tomorrow what you can do today, the early bird gets the worm—start to have less influence on you. You begin to realize it's okay to relax, and to do nothing, and even to go to bed early just for the ease of it.

66. Throw Out Everything
But the Aspirin

Several years ago we were in New York City on a business trip in the middle of winter, and I came down with a doozie of a cold. I didn't have time to run to a pharmacy to stock up on my usual supply of cold medicine. All I had with me was aspirin, so that's what I took to get me through. The cold lasted three days, then it was gone. Period.

I couldn't believe it. My colds have *always* lasted ten days to two weeks. Always. But then, I've always taken cold medicines. I began to wonder if there was a connection here. Did my colds last longer because I used cold remedies?

Next time I got a cold I resisted the temptation to turn to my usual cold relievers. I took only aspirin instead. Once again, the cold lasted only a few days.

I've discussed this idea with literally dozens of friends and associates, and many of them have started using aspirin in place of cold medicines with the same positive results I had. In addition to its use as a pain reliever, aspirin is now thought to prevent heart attacks in men, reduce the risk of certain types of strokes, reduce mortality among heart attack patients, reduce fevers, stop aches and inflammation, prevent gum disease, prevent high blood pressure in pregnant women, and prevent the recurrence of migraines.

I am the first to admit that this brief history does not constitute a scientific study of this phenomenon. But I was pleased to see a recent news item which supports my findings. According to this report, medical experts have told a House subcommittee in Washington that antihistamines, found in most over-the-counter cold medicines, are ineffective and pose unnecessary health and safety risks. They are urging the Food and Drug Administration (FDA) to withdraw antihistamines from cold medications.

In another recent report, the FDA declared flatly that hundreds of ingredients in over-the-counter medications simply don't work.

Perhaps it's time to approach your medicine cabinet with a heavy hand. Think seriously about getting rid of everything but the aspirin. That means throwing out the eye drops, ear salves, heartburn relievers, stomach coatings, hemorrhoidal preparations, and all the other products, including prescription drugs like sleeping pills and tranquilizers, that we Americans spend billions of dollars a year on.

If your eyes are bloodshot, instead of using Visine, which only masks the symptoms, figure out what is causing your eyes to be bloodshot; then stop doing it. If you've got heart-burn, lay off the pepperoni pizza, or get out of that stressful job.

There are no doubt dozens of medications we could do without if we just changed the way we live, so that the problems go away and eliminate the symptoms.

67. Create Your Own Rituals

 ✍

The type of ritual I'm referring to here is any special thing you can do on a regular basis that you look forward to, and that you think about with a happy heart.

I have a friend who has developed a special ritual for getting up in the morning. She wakes up a few minutes before daybreak and makes herself a special cup of tea, just the way she likes it with milk and honey. Then, winter or summer, rain or shine, she takes her tea and the huge comforter from her bed out to her screened porch. There, wrapped in her toastie blanket, she sips her tea and watches the sights and listens to the sounds of dawn. She never lets anything interfere with this quiet, sacred time. She knows that even if the rest of the day turns hectic, she'll have one memory of something being exactly the way she likes it.

It's possible that you've been working so hard and moving so fast that you haven't taken the time to incorporate some personalized moments into your day. If that's the case, take some time right now to think about a few special rituals you could create either on your own or with your family that would make each day memorable. And then start doing them.

68.   Learn to Laugh

Probably the best-known study of the effects of laughter on our lives and on our health is Norman Cousins's, described in his book, *Anatomy of an Illness.*

Mr. Cousins suffered from a rare connective tissue disease which left him completely debilitated. Finding no cure or respite through modern medical treatment, he decided to heal himself with laughter. He went to bed, fortified with every humorous movie and book he could get his hands on. It worked. His cure was remarkable, though little understood, or indeed explored, by the traditional medical community.

As children, we laugh naturally, but we gradually lose that skill as we become adults. It seems as we've moved faster and faster on the fast track, we've moved further and further away from our natural ability to laugh and have fun. Happily, laughter, like riding a bike, is a skill that can be easily relearned.

We are fortunate in our community to have an internationally known laughter therapist, Dr. Annette Goodheart, who offers a set of audio and video tapes on laughter, and who teaches courses and seminars around the world on how to laugh. She's been teaching these classes for over fifteen years, and they are always fully booked.

Laughter therapy is becoming more popular as practitioners learn the many benefits of this skill. If there are no classes in your community where you can learn how to laugh again, write for information on Dr. Goodheart's program—it may be offered in your area. (See below.)

Or think about the kinds of things that make you laugh, such as your favorite writers or comedians or cartoonists. Then stock up on books or tapes that you know will make you laugh, and watch or listen to them regularly, especially in times of stress. Or pick up one of those audio tapes that consists of solid laughter. Perhaps you have friends who make you laugh. If so, arrange to spend more time with them.

Laughter reduces stress, relieves tension, and soothes the angry heart. Just imagine how much simpler your life would be if you learned to respond to stressful situations with laughter rather than with frustration, or anger, or resentment.

For a brochure describing Dr. Goodheart's audio and video tapes, or for information regarding her seminars, write: Annette Goodheart, Ph.D., 635 N. Alisos St., Santa Barbara, CA 93103. (805) 966-0025.

69. Learn Yoga

Yoga is another technique, either by itself or in combination with meditation, that will help you simplify your life.

The principles of hatha (physical) yoga have been practiced for centuries because of the increased vitality, reduced fatigue, improved efficiency, enhanced concentration, and the serenity and peace of mind they generate. Yoga can be learned by people of all ages. It will strengthen, firm, tone, and shape your body, in addition to quieting your mind.

I had the good fortune years ago to study yoga with a yoga adept. I have used yoga consistently over the years for the physical, mental, and psychic benefits it provides. Once you have learned a sufficient number of the basic positions, they are easy to maintain and practice throughout your life. If you find from time to time you can't fit them all into your schedule, completing just a few of the stretching positions, combined with the proper yoga breathing, will produce obvious positive results.

Yoga is easy to learn, either through books and video tapes, which are readily available, or through class or private instruction, which is offered in most communities.

The combination of the yoga positions and the yoga breathing, by their very nature, will help you to slow down your hectic pace.

70. Learn to Meditate

All my life, though I have been attracted to the idea of meditation, I have resisted actually doing it. I was seldom able to sit still long enough. Now that I've simplified my life, meditation has become an important part of my regular routine. Many people have just the opposite experience: once they have learned to meditate, they find they gradually begin to simplify their lives. Whether you simplify first, and then learn to meditate, or start meditating, and begin to simplify, or even start both processes at the same time, you'll find meditation an effective way to maintain a simple life.

This is not to say that learning to meditate is easy, nor are the results necessarily immediate. But both the physical and psychological benefits of a sustained meditation program are well known and well documented. They include a much greater ability to deal with the everyday problems we all face, and a calmness and serenity that result from few other disciplines. Most people also find that meditation produces more energy, more restful sleep, an increased ability to concentrate, and an overall feeling of well-being.

There are many excellent books and tapes available which you can use to learn how to meditate. Some easy and effective methods are described in the little book, *How to Meditate,* by Lawrence LeShan. (Available in paperback from Bantam Books.)

Learning to meditate will give you a new understanding of your life, and will help you get clear on exactly how you want to live it.

71. Slow Down to the Posted Speed Limit

I was taught to drive in my youth by a professional race car driver. This may or may not have anything to do with the fact that I've always driven fast. I considered this an asset when I got onto the fast track, where it seemed as though everyone else was moving, both on foot and on wheels, at breakneck speeds. I was several years into our simplicity program before I realized that, while I had slowed down in almost every other area of my life, I was still driving as though I were on a race course.

I decided to change my driving style; I've learned to drive more slowly. Doing so has given me a whole new appreciation for driving, since I now have the opportunity to see and hear and feel more when I'm behind the wheel. And I'm more patient with other drivers, which has reduced the stress of driving. Paradoxically, it seems that slowing my driving speed has given me more time; more time to think, more time to reflect, and more time to enjoy life.

Once you slow down your driving pace, you'll no longer have to wonder why the driver in front of you is always traveling slower than you are.

Six

Your Personal Life

72. Clean Up Your Relationships

～

Creating a simple life isn't always simple. Some steps, like stopping the junk mail or throwing out everything but the aspirin, are easy and can be accomplished in a matter of minutes. Others, like moving to a smaller home or cleaning up your relationships, can take much longer and be among the most difficult things you ever have to do.

I'm referring to an impossible marriage or a relationship that isn't going anywhere, and that is causing you stress or pain. If you're in such a relationship, and you've tried to fix it and you can't, get out. If you can't come to that decision on your own, then get help. Talk to a therapist, or join a support group of people who are committed to your happiness and well-being. If you can't find such a group, then form one of your own. Meeting on a regular basis with people who are going through similar problems, and who are committed to growth, can provide a powerful impetus for you to get out of a dysfunctional relationship.

Cleaning up relationships applies to friends, too. Perhaps it's time to think about moving on from a friendship that no longer works for you. Ending a friendship, unlike ending a marriage, doesn't necessarily require a major confrontation or discussion. Depending on your history together, sometimes it's easier to retreat and simply fade out of someone else's life.

When you think about it, the *getting out* of a difficult relationship can be relatively easy. It is the *deciding* to get out that is often the difficult part. No other thing you could possibly do will simplify your life as quickly or as completely as getting out of a relationship that isn't working.

73.   Just Be Yourself

Have you ever stopped to think about how much energy you spend—and how much you complicate your life—by pretending to be someone other than who you are? We all do it. It's part of being human, and it was also a big part of the fast-paced life-style of the 1980s.

A good exercise is to sit down and go through all the major areas of your life and decide how each would be different if the only person you had to impress was you. Would you have a different career? What kind of house would you live in? Would you drive a different car? How would you dress? How would you spend your spare time? Would you be married to the person you're married to? Would you have the same friends?

Often we assume various layers of pretense not so much out of our own needs, but because of someone else's. How often are we untrue to ourselves because of the pressures of our family, the demands of our mate, the entreaties of our children? If your life-style reflects someone else's idea of how your life should be, take a few moments to imagine how much simpler it would be if you dropped the pretense and learned to just be yourself.

74. Trust Your Intuition

Have you ever found yourself getting into a situation that you just *knew* was not right for you? There were no doubt all kinds of "reasons" you could put down on paper that pointed toward going ahead with it, but there was something about it that just didn't feel good. If you listened to your intuition, you were probably glad later; if you didn't, you were probably sorry.

All of us come equipped with a still, small voice inside. Unfortunately, our life-styles have become so fast-paced and hectic that many of us have forgotten how to listen to it.

For years, whenever I was faced with a major decision, I would make a list of all the pros and cons, and then make my decision accordingly and, I always thought, logically. Oftentimes, logic had nothing to do with it. One of the things I've learned by slowing down is that, if I'm listening to my intuition, I don't have to make a list, I just *know* what I should do.

I have a friend who, when he can't decide between course A or course B, simply decides on one or the other—it doesn't matter which one—*then* he listens for the small voice which tells him whether he's happy with that decision. He has made a special point of teaching this method to his kids so they can get an early start on learning to trust their intuition.

Uncluttering your life (#1), learning to say no (#84), spending one day a month in solitude (#77), making an annual retreat (#79) and many of the other ideas in this book will contribute to slowing down your pace, and help you get in touch with your intuition. Learning to trust it will help keep your life in balance.

75.   If It's Not Easy,
Don't Do It

One of the many positive changes to come out of our simplification program is that I've finally learned that if something is difficult, it's better not to do it.

Many of us grew up with the misguided belief that if something is not going right, a business transaction, a partnership, or any kind of endeavor, all we had to do was work harder at it, and somehow we could solve it. Holding on to that belief has kept millions of people in difficult life choices, and has created a lot of unhappiness that could be avoided. Obviously, there is a difference between hard work that produces wonderful and satisfying results, and hard work that you just know is never going to get you anywhere.

You can't fit a square peg into a round hole. It takes courage to realize that something you've been working on, perhaps for a long time, just isn't right and to walk away from it. When I look back on my life I can see that the things that have worked out well were, for the most part, relatively easy; and the things that didn't work out well were, for the most part, difficult; they were simply not meant to be. I've learned that if it's not working, it's best just to move on, and to put my energies elsewhere.

Think how simple your life would be if you eliminated the difficult things—the things that probably weren't meant to be anyway—and concentrated on doing what was easy.

76. Stop Trying to Change People

I have a good friend who got into an awful mess a few years back from which she is still trying to extricate herself. But, in fact, she hasn't been trying nearly as hard as I have. I've spent a lot of frustrating time and energy over the years attempting to get her to see how she could change her life for the better. The solutions to her problems were so obvious—at least to me! The bottom line is that, though she pays lip service to wanting to change, she is really not all that interested.

One of the things that has become clear to me since I've started to slow down is that people do what they want to do. Understanding that has made it possible for me to see the fine line between being supportive and getting in the way. When it comes right down to it, we can't change other people. They change when they're good and ready. Ultimately, we all have to get out of our own predicaments. Most often what people really want is a supportive ear. This includes kids and spouses.

Now I just listen. Boy, has that simplified my life. And it has freed up a lot of energy to spend in more enjoyable and more productive pursuits.

77. Spend One Day a Month in Solitude

∽

If you already spend a fair amount of time alone, or if you've made sufficient changes in your life so that you are out from under the pressures that once made it so complicated, you may already be getting all the solitude you need.

But if your days are full of family, friends, traffic, noise, demands, requests, pressures, deadlines, schedules, and an endless parade of people, you may want to think about spending a day or possibly a weekend each month by yourself, completely away from the everyday distractions that complicate your life.

Spending a day in solitude can mean doing anything from taking a hike up a mountain trail, to sitting quietly on a park bench. It can mean a day spent wandering through art museums or art galleries, or a day browsing in the stacks at your local library. While it doesn't necessarily mean getting away from people, it definitely means getting away from people you know who are likely to make demands on you.

Spending time away from the constant barrage of pressures we face can get us back in touch with what is real, and can help to alleviate the tensions of everyday life. After all, freeing ourselves from the pressures of modern living is a major part of what simplifying is all about.

Hint: If you're not in the habit of taking time for yourself, you may need to explain to your mate and/or family members what you plan to do and your desire to spend time alone. It's important that those close to you understand your need for solitude so they won't feel left out or rejected.

78. Teach Your Kids the Joy of Solitude

‿

As anyone who has children knows, the pressures on kids today are enormous. Alcohol, drugs of every variety, sex, AIDS, gangs, guns, and violence, not to mention the constant stimulus and often ear-shattering intrusions from inane television, tempestuous movies, rock music, rap singers, coffeehouses, computer games, and video arcades. How can a young person find peace of mind today, learn to get in touch with his own feelings, or find out what is important to *him*?

One way is for kids to learn at an early age how to seek out quiet time on their own. As you are learning to spend some time in solitude, teach your kids to do the same. Take them on nature hikes or on camping trips away from the continuous jangle of urban living. Make a ritual of watching a beautiful sunset with them.

Or teach them how to spend a quiet afternoon at home. Set up a regular time in their week where they can be away from the unremitting influence of their peers, as well as away from the pandemonium of the electronic age. Fortify them with good books (but no TV) and thoughtful meditative exercises they can do, so they get in the habit of personal reflection, and of seeking answers within their own hearts.

Once your children learn the joy of solitude, it'll be a gift they can carry with them throughout their lives. And, imagine how much simpler your life will be when your children, in learning to enjoy their own solitude, learn to appreciate your desire for solitude as well.

79. Do a Retreat
Once a Year

If you find it difficult to schedule some regular time for solitude, consider doing an annual retreat. I have found few things as good for the soul as slipping off on my own for three or four days to get away not only from the material clutter we all face, but from the emotional, psychic, and social clutter as well.

It's surprisingly easy to do. It doesn't have to be connected to any type of religious organization. A spa or resort hotel-type retreat can be very effective. But going off on your own to contemplate your life doesn't have to be expensive. One of the most refreshing retreats I've done recently was a camping trip in the mountains. It was a much welcomed opportunity to get in touch with nature as well as with my psyche. It is amazing what a couple of days surrounded by the beauty and peace and quiet of nature can do for your perspective.

Also, there are dozens of small and often elegant retreat houses that offer simple but comfortable accommodations for three or four nights at very reasonable rates. Many of these are former monasteries or convents that have been converted into nondenominational retreat centers. Their directors are committed to providing a quiet setting for personal and spiritual growth.

Sanctuaries, by Jack and Marcia Kelly (published by Bell Tower in both an East Coast and West Coast edition) is an excellent source of information on lodgings, monasteries, and retreat houses around the country.

80. Keep a Journal

Keeping a journal is another effective way to stay in touch with how you want to live your life.

A journal can be as loose or as structured as you wish to make it. It can include random reflections and ideas about the world and your place in it, or it can be a formal method of keeping a daily record of your thoughts and feelings as a means toward spiritual growth. It can be something you write in every day, or you can use it sporadically as the mood and the need arise. It can be a dream journal, an idea journal, a diet journal, a creativity journal, an anger journal, or a health journal. It can be full of thoughts you want to share with others, or as private as you want to make it.

Many local community college and adult education programs offer courses in journal writing. Being involved in a journal-writing class is an excellent way to work with other people who are learning how to use this technique effectively in their lives, and to share ideas on new and different approaches that could work for you.

Or just pick up a pen and a notebook and develop your own journal-writing system to help you keep in touch with what's important to you.

81. Do One Thing at a Time

We're all familiar with the image of the modern American yuppie barreling down the highway in his BMW while talking on the car phone to his office and pulling an urgent memo off the car fax. He's in the process of closing a major deal with the executive sitting in the front seat next to him, assuming he can get to the sales presentation meeting at his client's office across town on time.

Or the young executive who's having a relaxing weekend at home in front of the TV with her family. She's changing the baby's diaper and talking to her boss long distance, while keeping her mother-in-law on call waiting. As soon as she's off the phone(s), she'll be wrapping up the game of Go Fish with her three-year-old so the kids can finish their snack before the ten dinner guests arrive for the business meeting she's hosting for her husband.

We each could tell our own version of this "gotta do it all" madness that has pervaded our lives. Do we really get more done by trying to do everything at once? Maybe. Does it *really* matter? Probably not. Are we happier at this frenetic pace?

Most definitely not. Can we do anything about it? Yes. Just as we gradually learned to do ten things at once, we can gradually learn to do one thing at a time.

Start with a list. Not the HAVE TO DO TODAY list you have in your Day Runner, but a *new* list of the things that really matter. Cut the list in half, then pick the most important thing, and do it. Then, and only then, go down the list, doing each thing, one at a time. As much as possible, allow no distractions, no interruptions. After the first couple of weeks, consider it a major accomplishment if you are able to cut in half again the number of things you feel you *have* to do each day.

With a little discipline and regular self-checks, you can learn to do one thing at a time. And do it better. And be happier doing it.

82. Do Nothing

∞

Do nothing. It sounds so easy. Then I think back to my frenetic life-style of a couple of years ago, before I decided to simplify. I had to-do lists a mile long, nonstop appointments, and phone calls around the clock. Every moment of my day was scheduled, even my sleep time. And I remembered how long it took for me to get to a point where I could actually *do nothing*. It took a while. It's more difficult than it sounds.

If you're not in the habit of doing nothing, how do you start? Start with an hour. Maybe a lunch hour, or an hour at the end of your workday, or perhaps with the extra hour you have once you start getting up an hour earlier (#64).

If you start with your lunch hour, go to a quiet place and just sit. This is not the reading a book, or the talking with friends, or the working on your knitting kind of doing nothing. This is not about meditation. The idea is to just *be* with whatever is going on in your head without having to *do* anything about it.

Another good way to learn to do nothing is to stay in your office or your home, surrounded by all the things you should be doing, and do nothing. If you've not done this before, it may take several tries at it to get past the guilt or the almost uncontrollable urge to start doing something.

Gradually, you can start increasing the time you do nothing, until you build up to at least a half day or a full day once a month, or more if possible. Once you've learned to do nothing, you'll be amazed at the clarity it will bring to your life, or to whatever project you're working on. It's unbelievably refreshing.

Now, at the very least, I have one or two days a month where I do nothing. Few things will put a hectic, over-scheduled life-style into perspective faster than learning this skill. I urge you to get started, and do nothing.

83. Take Time to Watch the Sunset

Sunset has always been one of my favorite times of day. Before I simplified my life, I was frequently too busy to enjoy it. Now that my world is simpler, I almost never miss what is regularly one of the most spectacular shows on earth.

There's something so captivating about the setting sun, especially when weather and atmospheric conditions help to create dramatic cloud formations and brilliant colors that give your whole world a different hue. Seen in the light of the setting sun, our problems seem minor, even if only for a few moments.

The wonderful thing about sunset, and much the same can be said for sunrise, is that it happens every day, and even if the sunset itself is not spectacular, it marks the beginning of the end of another day. It's a great time to pause and take notice. Teach your kids to enjoy the beauty of sunrises and sunsets, too. It's a very inexpensive show and it's a whole lot better for them than television.

84.   Just Say No

One of the things I promised myself when we decided to simplify our lives was to reduce my social commitments to people beyond the circle of my immediate family and friends. I've finally reached a point where, if someone asks me to do something I don't want to do or spend an evening with people I don't have any interest in being with, I simply say no. Thank you, but no.

My weekdays are devoted, for the most part, to my work, and, unavoidably, there are deadlines and obligations I have to meet. But my evenings and weekends are my own. They have become sacred, and learning to say no to things I don't want to do—especially those things I have always felt I *should* do—has kept them inviolate.

If you have a problem saying no, go back and read *When I Say No, I Feel Guilty,* by Manuel J. Smith. This classic best-seller from the 1970s will give you the verbal tools you need to reduce your commitments and make your time your own again.

85. If You Can't Say No, Prevaricate

∽

Have you ever found yourself trapped at a social gathering you didn't want to attend in the first place because you were caught off guard when the hostess invited you? The truth is you didn't really *want* to go, but you didn't have any other plans, *and* you didn't have an excuse ready. It's happened to most of us.

I have a friend who for years just couldn't say no. Sally is a strong, dynamic woman who runs a successful business and has never had a problem managing a staff of twenty people, dealing assertively with suppliers, or meeting on an equal footing with corporate executives. But when it came to her social life, she'd always been a pushover. She knew it, but she couldn't bear to hurt people's feelings.

However, she recently found herself fidgeting through yet another dinner party. She realized that if she'd been prepared with a socially acceptable excuse when Martha had called to invite her, she'd be at home at that moment cozying up on the sofa with a good book. She decided right there, in the middle of Martha's Canary Islands cassoulet, that she'd never again say yes when she wanted to say no.

So she's learned to prevaricate. She drew up a list of all-purpose excuses which she keeps by her home and office phones. Now, when people call with invitations to gatherings she has no interest in, she's prepared. She has also developed the habit of keeping a couple of excuses on the tip of her tongue to ward off acquaintances she might run into on the street or in the grocery checkout line. She's finally reconciled to the fact that just because she may like someone, she doesn't have to give up her free time to be with them, unless she wants to.

She's learned that a simple excuse is the best: "Thanks, Martha, but I've got plans for Saturday night." And she's also learned not to add, "Maybe next time," because she knows the Marthas of the world will take her at her word.

Needless to say, her social life is dwindling rapidly, but she has more free time than she's ever had to do the things that really matter to her.

86. Resign from Any Organizations Whose Meetings You Dread

∽

While I've never been much of a joiner, Gibbs went through a stage in his life when he'd join any group that invited him. One of the things he did when we started to simplify was to resign from the groups where he found his heart was no longer in it.

It's amazing how quickly memberships—and the accompanying obligations and guilts—can pile up. The financial drain—with countless dues and assessments and overpriced rubber-chicken dinners deadened by Worst Speech Ever contests—is one thing. But the frustration of working with often disorganized and fanatical amateurs, or trying desperately to make small talk with people whose only connection to your life is through a single, narrowly focused interest, can be emotionally and psychologically debilitating.

Here is his advice for getting out. Take all your membership cards (you may be appalled at how many there are). Make two stacks. The smaller, maybe nonexistent, pile consists of organizations that meet at least two of three criteria:

1. Membership is a professional imperative.

2. You actually look forward to their meetings.

3. You never find yourself apologizing for being a member.

Resign from all the rest. Or if you can't bring yourself to resign, just let your memberships quietly lapse. You'll find you've reclaimed a significant chunk of your free time.

87. Learn to Reinterpret the Past

∽

Do you ever find yourself reliving some upsetting event or circumstance of your life, feeling you just can't seem to get over it? This could be anything from an altercation with a co-worker to the dissolution of your marriage. It could have happened years ago, or only yesterday. You keep thinking about it, wishing you had done things differently. It haunts you, but agonizing over it doesn't seem to help.

One of the things I've been able to do as a result of slowing down the pace of my life is to stop reliving the past. I've come to realize that, when you get right down to it, there are no mistakes; there are no wrong decisions. I've gotten into the habit of interpreting the events of my life—whether apparently "good" or "bad"—as powerful circumstances that, no matter what the temporary outcome, will ultimately get me where I want to go.

Constantly reliving past events only complicates your life. Reinterpreting them as positive steps forward, and then moving on, will keep things simple.

88. Change Your Expectations

The 1980s created sometimes unrealistic goals and expectations that we all felt we could or should live up to. It was taken for granted that we would strive for the biggest houses, the fastest cars, the best jobs, the highest paychecks, the most promising futures, the happiest marriages, the most organized households, the brightest kids in the best schools, the latest fashions, and all the space-age gadgets and toys money could buy. Many people have worked harder and harder and feel they haven't achieved all those expectations. Many people have exceeded their expectations, but it hasn't made them happy.

We have an acquaintance who is stuck in his expectations. He's got the big house, the big car, the club memberships, and the high-powered career, but he's miserable. He doesn't like what he does for a living, but he can't imagine giving it up because it's the job that makes it possible for him to keep the big house, the big car, and the big life-style that he feels he's "earned" and is entitled to.

Much of our own simplification program, in fact, revolved

around changing our expectations. For Gibbs and me, and a lot of other people, the big life-style wasn't as advertised. When we moved across country so we could get away from the four-hour commute and live where we worked (#51), we had to change our expectations about our career goals. We wondered at the time if we had lowered them, but the extra four hours that the move added to our day, and the tremendous improvement in the quality of that time, more than made up for any loss in terms of career advancement. And, as it turned out, both of us experienced career changes that are now much more satisfying, though very different, from our original expectations.

If you feel you haven't achieved all those goals, or if you exceeded them and you still aren't happy, maybe it's time to admit that the life of the superachiever isn't necessarily what it was cracked up to be. Hanging on to the expectations of the 1980s is a surefire way to complicate your life. Letting go of them, and establishing your own priorities, will greatly simplify your life.

89. Review Your Life Regularly to Keep It Simple

‿

Maintaining a simple life requires a certain amount of vigilance. It is not realistic to go through the steps to simplify your life and then think it will automatically stay simple. First of all, many of us have been in the habit of consuming and expanding for some years now, and old habits die hard. Second, our culture is not structured to readily accommodate those who choose to simplify. There are constant messages from the media, our families, our friends, and the Joneses urging us to buy this new gadget or try that new toy or, in one way or another, get back on the fast track. Most of these messages seem irresistible. Some are valid; some are not. It's your choice.

We have friends who decided to simplify their eating habits. They were both dedicated gourmet chefs and owned practically every piece of cooking equipment known to man. When they went through the uncluttering routine in their kitchen (#1), they got rid of, among other things, the wine-making apparatus, the electric tortilla press, the combination capuccino/espresso brewer/milk steamer, the pasta maker, and the institution-sized mixer with 42 attachments. They spent many months rejoicing in their newfound liberation from cooking-equipment catalogs.

Then, before they knew what had happened, they woke up one day to realize that they had replaced the wine gear with a juicer, the pasta maker and tortilla press with an electric breadmaker, and the 42-attachment mixer with a seed-sprouting contraption that took up half their deck space.

Simple? Not exactly, and it shows you what can happen when you're not paying attention.

Seven

Special Issues
for Women

In the movie *Tootsie,* Dustin Hoffman plays an actor who impersonates a female actress in order to get an acting job. He has just come home from a shopping spree where he has purchased all the accouterments he needs for his role as a woman: wigs, hair rollers, makeup, nail polish, jewelry, shoes, handbags, etc. As he is putting on his wig and makeup, he comments to his roommate that he never realized how much time and energy and money women have to spend just to make themselves presentable. Boy, isn't that the truth?

There is no doubt about it, women in our culture are high-maintenance. I decided to take a cold hard look at the routine I've always gone through to be presentable. I came up with some specific things women can do to get to low-maintenance, and I've included them in this separate section, written just for women. Men, for the most part, are already low-maintenance.

90. Ten Minutes to Drop-Dead Gorgeous

∽

I've always marveled at how Gibbs could get dressed and look totally put together in less than half the time it took me to get ready for the same event. When we started simplifying our lives, I made it my personal goal to go from a standing start to drop-dead gorgeous in ten minutes or less. (I've got the ten minutes down pat; I'm still working on the drop-dead part.)

I started with my hair style. For most women the time-consuming part of getting dressed is the hair we've been brainwashed into believing has to be not only shampooed, but conditioned, color rinsed, moussed, spritzed, gelled, blow-dried, extended, enhanced, straightened, or curled, and then sprayed before we can go out the front door.

Men have hair styles that make it possible for them to wash their hair, run a comb through it, and go. Women can do that too. Years ago a hairdresser told me that every woman has at least one flattering low-maintenance easy-care hair style that is natural for her hair type and facial structure. It took some experimentation, but I found an easy-care hair style that works for me. Now, rather than the twenty to thirty minutes it used to take, my hair is clean and ready-to-go in five or six minutes.

Second, I changed my skin-cleansing habits. For years I was unable to pass a cosmetics counter without stocking up on the latest eight-step day-time-night-time-cleanser-moisturizer-scrub-softener-pore reducer-skin enhancer-line eliminator program for my sensitive skin. Fortunately, I recently was stranded on a deserted island without my usual array of skin products. All I had was a sponge, water, and a natural skin cream. After three weeks on this routine my skin had never looked better.

Now, all I use is a sponge and water for cleansing and a few drops of light moisturizer. I can't tell you what a relief it is not only to have a system that is easy and that works, but to be rid of all those half-used jars of goop that for years have cluttered up my drawers and countertops.

Another thing you can do is rethink your use of makeup. Have you ever seen a face that was improved by the tons of makeup cosmetic manufacturers would have us wear—all with the purpose of making us look like we're not wearing makeup? Ask the men in your life. Most will tell you they prefer women with a natural look and a smile.

While you're at it, be sure to include your daughters in

your natural looks program. Just imagine the hassles you could save them—and the positive self-esteem you could build—if they never became enchanted with the beauty-in-a-jar myth.

You may have to change your expectations (#88) to get to low-maintenance, but once you do, you'll wonder how you ever put up with your old routine.

91. Kick Off Your High Heels— and Keep Them Off

Few of the dictates of fashion have been more universally limiting and damaging to women than high-heeled shoes. Any podiatrist will tell you that women who regularly wear high heels suffer not only from deformed, bunioned, and callused feet, but from myriad other maladies, including calf, knee, and back problems. And yet, women continue to wear heels, all in the name of fashion.

Isn't it fortunate that current styles allow at least some room for individuality, and that it's possible to wear comfortable, low-heeled or flat-heeled shoes and still make a fashion statement? Yes, it's true that many men find high heels sexy. (That, after all, is why we put ourselves through the torture and inconvenience of heels.) But if you really want to simplify your life, and you're still wearing high heels because the men around you find women in heels attractive, maybe it's time to change the people you spend time with.

Aside from the discomfort, having high heels in your closet raises the complexity of your wardrobe to another level. Think how simple it would be if all the shoes in your closet were the same heel height. That's one of the primary reasons men's wardrobes are inherently simpler than women's: They can wear any number of different shoes, in total comfort, with the same suit or pair of slacks without having to worry about the length of the pant leg.

After you've been away from high-heeled shoes for a while, few things will look more pathetic than a woman mincing down the street in high heels. And you'll know that if her feet aren't hurting her now, they soon will be.

92. Take Off Your Plastic Nails and Throw Out the Nail Polish

ᔕ

One of the most complicating and time-consuming aspects of the high-tech dress-for-success mode of the 1980s was the highly polished, brightly colored, fake nails craze. When you stop to think about it, it's hard to imagine any cosmetic procedure we've ever put ourselves through that takes more time, costs more money, does more damage to ourselves with toxic fumes and the potential for nail fungus and other problems, and creates more havoc for the environment for less benefit to anyone than fake and/or highly polished nails.

Obviously, spending several hours each week surrounded by noxious fumes while having acrylic nails cemented layer by layer to your fingertips is not compatible with the simple life. Thank goodness, the vampire look is out. If, like me and millions of other women, you have indulged in this practice, it may be time to start developing an appreciation for the simple beauty of neatly filed, closely trimmed, unpainted nails. Just imagine never again having to go through the gyrations of pulling on a pair of nylon stockings after having just touched up your nail polish.

93. Stop Carrying a Purse the Size of the QE2

᳥

If you want to simplify your fashion statement, your purse should be the most inconspicuous item you have. Preferably it should be invisible.

If you feel you must carry a purse, make it a very small one with a shoulder strap, so you can keep your hands free, and just big enough to hold an ID, some money, and your lipstick. What else do you really need for getting back and forth to work or going out for an evening? Any other items you think you can't live without can be kept in the glove compartment of your car and/or stowed in your desk drawer at the office.

Of course, the slacks and skirts and jackets of your simple wardrobe (#22) will have pockets, and you can get by on most outings by stashing some cash and possibly your lipstick there.

If you've never experienced the freedom of not having to lug around a huge purse full of items you don't need and seldom use—a so-called handbag that in almost every instance detracts from whatever you're wearing—now is a good time to start.

94. Minimize Your Accessories

ᔕ

If there is one variable that can make or break a fashion statement for women, it's accessories. Once again, men have it easy: All they have to worry about is a tie, possibly a tie pin, a watch, a briefcase, and shoes (which, because they are almost always the same color and height, aren't, strictly speaking, an accessory). Women have to deal with earrings, necklaces, bracelets, brooches, watches, scarves, ties, belts, glasses, handbags, a briefcase, occasionally a hat, stockings, and shoes of every conceivable color and height.

Because the variety of accessories is unlimited, and because the appropriate combination of these items is an art form that few women have mastered, most of us have a problem getting it right, particularly when it comes to shoes and purses. How many times have you seen an otherwise wonderfully combined outfit ruined by shoes of the wrong height, or a handbag that simply doesn't work with the rest of the ensemble? Gucci and Louis Vuitton and other "initialed" bags are the worst offenders. They seldom go with *anything*.

The classic fashion statements that have endured the test of time have always been the simplest. Getting rid of your handbag and kicking off your high heels will go a long way toward simplifying your look. Cutting back your jewelry to a couple of simple but elegant pairs of earrings, and eliminating most of the rest of the accessories, will make the job even easier.

Eight

Hard-Core
Simplicity

95. Rent Rather Than Own

Over the past fifty years we've been brainwashed into believing that owning our own home is the only way to go. In a recent survey conducted by the National Association of Realtors, 87 percent of the respondents said that owning their own home was the most important element in fulfilling the "American dream." Home ownership is valued more than a happy marriage, an interesting job, high pay, or even having a lot of money.

Considering the high cost of home ownership these days, maybe it is time to reconsider that philosophy.

We have friends who, like us, have recently made some major changes in their lives. They sold their home, got rid of their cars and most of their stuff, quit their jobs, and spent two years traveling around the world. They took the equity they had built up in their home, and used it to generate income to support their greatly reduced life-style.

When they came back from their travels, they initially considered buying another, smaller home. But they decided to rent an apartment instead. Not only can they now rent a comfortable apartment for much less than it would cost to own comparable space, they want the freedom of not owning. Should they decide to take off and do some more traveling, they don't want to be trapped by a slow market and not be able to sell when they're ready to go.

But, to their surprise, the biggest reason for not owning a home is the emotional and psychological freedom it gives them. Contrary to what they had believed all these years, home ownership had become a burden rather than a security. If your home is costing you more time, energy and money than you're willing to pay, consider renting. It could greatly simplify your life.

96. Get Rid of Your Cars

We have friends who live in San Francisco. Several years ago they sold their cars because they were just too much trouble. In a city like San Francisco, parking is always a problem as well as a major expense. And they didn't really need even one car, let alone two of them. They live close enough to their offices so they can both walk to work. They love the forced exercise and the fresh air. They also love not having to fight big-city traffic. In a pinch or in inclement weather, they can catch a bus.

Now, rather than running all over town, they do all their shopping within walking distance of their home. The money they save on gas, parking, insurance, taxes, registration fees, and maintenance they can use to rent a car if they want to get away for the weekend or if they need a car for some other short-term purpose. After years of being psychologically dependent on cars, they feel a tremendous sense of freedom in not having to worry about the problems of owning a car. Now that they don't have the "convenience" of a car, they spend a lot less time running around on unnecessary jaunts, and they can spend that time doing things they really want to do.

Obviously, if you live in the suburbs and work in the city, and if public transportation is unreliable or nonexistent, giving up your car probably wouldn't make a whole lot of sense. But if you could rearrange your life so that you didn't *need* a car, it could be a major step in simplifying your life.

97. Get Rid of Your Phone

As a teenager, I loved the telephone. It always rang with such anticipation. As an adult, I look on the phone as a necessary inconvenience. However, now that I've developed the ability to not answer a ringing phone and to use the answering machine to monitor phone calls, having a phone in the house is at least tolerable. But I have a friend who came to look on the phone as a major intrusion in her life. She disconnected it entirely a couple of years ago and says she wouldn't have it any other way.

She is in sales and consequently spends most of her day talking on the phone. The last thing she wants to do at home in the evening and on the weekends is spend more time on the phone. She is able to conduct whatever personal phone business she needs to during the day, and her family and friends know that if they want to talk to her, they have to call her at the office. (It helps to have your own business; or a tolerant boss.)

Obviously this technique would not work for everyone. If you have children at home or aging parents who may need to reach out and touch you at a moment's notice, disconnecting the phone might create more problems than it would solve. But think about it. If your life-style is such that going without a phone at home wouldn't be inconvenient and, in fact, would create a sanctuary of peace and quiet, doing away with the telephone in your life could go a long way toward simplifying it.

98.   Stop Making the Bed

∽

If it's good enough to get out of, it's good enough to get into.

—AUNT MYRNA, 1953

If an unmade bed is good enough for Ralph Lauren, it's good enough for me.

—THE AUTHOR, 1993

There's no question housekeeping practices have become less rigid in the past forty years. Just look at the ads for bed linens. A few years back Ralph Lauren started making a very appealing case for the unmade bed, with all the sheets, dust ruffles, pillows, duvets, spreads, and coverlets that abound in the confusion of the unmade beds in his ads. In the perfection-personified *Leave It to Beaver* household of the fifties, Mrs. Cleaver—and no doubt your mother and mine—would never have *thought* of leaving a bed unmade. And Aunt

Myrna's philosophy was thought, by our family anyway, to be close to heresy.

But now, fortunately, times have changed. Who cares if the bed is left unmade? And who is going to see it? A good friend of mine, who is a firm believer in the unmade bed, has what I think is a wonderful response to anyone who might comment on the disarray of her bed: "Oh, we're just airing the linens."

I've adopted that philosophy totally. Not only is it simpler, but now, when I get out of bed in the morning and know I don't have to spend ten minutes making up the darn thing, it gives me the delight of feeling as though I'm getting away with a little something. It's a treat I can carry with me throughout the day. And besides, why would anyone spend all that money buying linens from a guy named Ralph, and then cover them up?

99. Get Rid of All the Extras

∽

When I started college, I threw out all my old emery boards and, in what seemed like an extravagance on my student budget, decided to go for broke and purchased a stainless nail file that was guaranteed to last a lifetime.

I was fond of that little file. I carried it back and forth across the country and around several continents for fifteen years.

Once I started generating some discretionary income, I splurged and bought half a dozen more stainless nail files. I wanted one in my handbag, one in my desk, one in the glove compartment, one in the nightstand, etc.

But then a curious thing happened. When I had only one nail file, I always knew where it was. As soon as I had several, I could never find a nail file when I needed one. Over the years, I've discovered that same phenomenon applies to many things.

For example, a person with one watch knows what time it is, but someone with two watches is never quite sure. And what's worse, he's become a collector. Now, not only does he have to deal with the maintenance and upkeep of the collection, but he also has to keep track of where each item in the collection is at any given moment.

In no time at all, having extra sets of things can get very complicated. I long ago got rid of the extra nail files, and more recently I've gotten rid of the extra eyeglasses, sunglasses, fountain pens, umbrellas, pocket knives, hammers, and all kinds of specialized tools, even the extra computers. It's made my life so much simpler.

100. Build a *Very*
Simple Wardrobe

‿

If you're *very* serious about simplicity, here is another fashion option you might want to consider.

A wealthy Wall Street financier is reputed to have developed the simplest wardrobe of all: he has half a dozen copies of one exquisitely tailored black three-piece suit, a couple of identical white shirts and silk ties, and a couple of pairs of black shoes. That's it. Year in and year out that's all he ever wears. His reasoning is that he has enough decisions to make each day without having to worry about what to wear too.

Think about it. This, or your own variation of this idea, could *really* simplify your life.